WHO
IS
THE
REAL
JESUS?

WHO
IS
THE
REAL
JESUS?

Discover the Evidence . . .

Decide for Yourself

Y-JESUS.COM

WinePressPublishing
Great Books, Defined.

ISBN 13: 978-1-4141-2065-2
ISBN 10: 1-4141-2065-6
Library of Congress Catalog Card Number: 2011924766

CONTENTS

ACKNOWLEDGMENTS

I AM INDEBTED to project director, Helmut Teichert, who has been instrumental in the development of this material since the initial collaboration with Dr. Bright and Dr. Brandt. Helmut set standards of excellence that guided the entire process. I am also indebted to Rick James and Eric Stanford for their professional collaboration in the writing and editing of this book.

Several others contributed to the preparation of this material, including Dr. Bill Bright, Dr. Henry Brandt, Dave Chapman, Dr. Bert Harned, and Dr. Ron Heine.

Dr. Bright's great desire to share the evidence for Jesus Christ with those who have intellectual questions led to his founding of Campus Crusade for Christ. Prior to his death, he enthusiastically endorsed the writing of this material, desiring it to have a worldwide impact. I am also thankful to Dr. Brandt who, along with Dr. Bright, shared a passion to present the evidence for Jesus Christ to as many people as possible.

Thanks also are in order to Dave Chapman for his many invaluable editing suggestions which significantly helped illustrate and clarify key points and concepts.

This book would never have been written without the inspiration and mentoring of Dr. Bert Harned, who has spent a lifetime sharing the truth about Jesus Christ and the purpose he can bring to our existence. I am one of many who has personally benefited from Bert's faithfulness in presenting this message.

Finally, I would like to thank my wife, Marianne, for inspiring me to summarize the evidence for Jesus Christ so that a young man seeking the truth would be able to clearly see the evidence and draw his own conclusions. Her patience during the lengthy writing process, as well as her insightful comments and suggestions, were indispensable in the development and editing of this material from beginning to completion.

—**Larry Chapman,**
General Editor

INTRODUCTION
The Jesus of History: Man or Myth?

TWO THOUSAND YEARS ago something happened that changed our world. According to ancient written testimonies, a man who was different from all others set foot on our planet. He claimed to be from beyond our world. His name was Jesus. The incredible feats and lofty words attributed to him have caused some to label him a myth—they believe he didn't exist. But the vast majority of scholars believe otherwise, acknowledging Jesus Christ as a real historical person.[1] [See endnote 1.]

After reading the New Testament accounts of Jesus, Albert Einstein, the great scientist, became convinced of Jesus' reality. Although Einstein was an agnostic, his awe for Jesus caused him to remark, "No one can read the Gospels without feeling the actual presence of Jesus. His personality pulsates in every word. No myth is filled with such life . . . . No man can deny the fact that Jesus existed, nor that his sayings are beautiful."[2] Virtually all leading secular historians, such as Will Durant and H. G. Wells, have been convinced of his reality.[3] Summing up the opinions of first-rank historians, Wells wrote of Jesus, "Here was a man. This part of the tale could not have been invented."[4]

Ancient history offers several clues about Jesus Christ. These clues come from archaeological discoveries, contemporary historical documents, and ancient New Testament manuscripts.

Archaeologists have discovered relics of names and places associated with Jesus. These discoveries include the synagogue in Capernaum where Jesus often taught, a stone with the name Pontius Pilate, the ossuary of Caiaphas—the High Priest who tried Jesus—and the recent discovery of first-century Nazareth, the town where Jesus lived as a child. Until that discovery, many skeptics had argued Jesus couldn't have lived in Nazareth since there had been no evidence of the town's existence in the first century. [See Y-Jesus. com / Evidence1.]

Evidence for Jesus has also been discovered in written documents dating as early as the first and second centuries. Within five years of Jesus' life, church creeds spoke of his crucifixion and resurrection. Furthermore, within 150 years of Jesus' life, forty-two authors mention him in their writings, including nine non-Christian sources. During that same time period, only ten authors mention Tiberius Caesar—the Roman emperor during Jesus' ministry.[5] [See endnote 5.] Yet no serious historian doubts the existence of Tiberius Caesar.

There is also more early documentary evidence for the existence of Jesus than for Alexander the Great. The historicity of Alexander the Great and his military conquests is drawn from only five ancient sources, none of whom were eyewitnesses. Although written four hundred years after Alexander, Plutarch's *Life of Alexander* is the primary account of his life. Of the twenty contemporary historical accounts on Alexander, not one survives. But regardless of the time-gap of several hundred years, historians are convinced that Alexander was a real man and that the essential details of what we read about his life are true. So how reliable are the historical accounts of Jesus?

The New Testament accounts are, of course, the primary record of Jesus' words and life. They claim to have been written by eyewitnesses. They record the words he spoke and the numerous miracles he performed. But could these accounts have been legendary like the sacred writings of so many other religions? Not according to most leading scholars who have analyzed them. C. S. Lewis, who taught literature at both Oxford and Cambridge, wrote, "Now as a literary historian,

I am perfectly convinced that the Gospels are not legends."[6]

However, books like Dan Brown's fictional work, *The Da Vinci Code,* argue that the original message about Jesus has been altered and his identity hijacked. Other authors have tried to capitalize on Brown's success with their own version of a Jesus conspiracy. But the evidence to support *The Da Vinci Code*'s assertion that the records of Jesus were changed simply isn't there, according to historians.[7] On the contrary, over 5,300 ancient New Testament manuscript copies provide a very accurate picture of what the apostles first wrote about Jesus.

Since thousands of these New Testament manuscripts exist, scholars are able to compare their words, applying the science of textual criticism to determine what the original documents said. New Testament scholar F. F. Bruce acknowledged, "There is no body of ancient literature in the world which enjoys such a wealth of good textual attestation as the New Testament."[8] This enormous wealth of early manuscript evidence strongly supports the reliability of the New Testament today. Although a few minor words are in question, the essential message of Jesus' life and words is clear and reliable.

Some critics have argued that the New Testament was written at least a hundred years later than the events they describe. If true, there would have been no eyewitness reports.

However, more recent evidence reveals a much earlier dating, well within the lifetime of the apostles who wrote them. One compelling discovery that stunned critics of the New Testament's reliability is a tiny fragment of a copy of John's Gospel dated AD 114–125.[9] The words on that copy of the original Gospel, as well as those on later manuscript copies, are virtually identical to the New Testament today. Regardless of the ongoing attacks on the New Testament from skeptics, the evidence for its reliability is well documented. [See Appendix B.]

Nevertheless, some remain skeptical about the miraculous nature of Jesus' birth, life, death, and resurrection spoken of in the New Testament.

Leading atheist Richard Dawkins wrote to his ten-year-old daughter, Juliet, about beliefs and evidence. In his counsel, Dawkins admonished Juliet to be skeptical of anything that can't be supported by evidence:

> Belief that there is a god or gods, belief in Heaven, . . . belief that Jesus never had a human father, belief that prayers are answered . . . not one of these beliefs is backed up by any good evidence.

Dawkins adamantly states in his letter to Juliet that there is no evidence to substantiate belief in Jesus Christ as divine. Yet he also counsels her to seek evidence before drawing her own conclusions.

> And, next time somebody tells you that something is true, why not say to them: "What kind of evidence is there for that?" And if they can't give you a good answer, I hope you'll think very carefully before you believe a word they say.
>
> Your loving Daddy[10]

Dawkins's advice to his daughter raises a good question: Why should we believe any of Jesus' miraculous deeds, particularly his resurrection from the dead? Tales of mythical gods such as Osiris, Tammuz, Adonis, and Horus dying and rising from the dead lead us to ask what's different about the account of Jesus' resurrection. That's a great question that needs to be answered by the evidence.

For one thing, an examination of the historical evidence reveals that the earliest of these alleged "parallel" accounts "appeared at least 100 years after the reports of Jesus' resurrection."[11] [See endnote 11.] "The ancient Egyptian cult of Osiris is the only account of a god who survived death that predates Christianity," but the mythical return to life of Osiris was "far different than Jesus' resurrection account."[12]

So, aside from the fact that a few similarities exist between accounts of certain ancient gods and Jesus Christ, the accusation that the Gospel accounts of Jesus were "copied" from these mythological religions has been demonstrated to be false. But that fact alone doesn't prove Jesus rose from the dead. To determine whether or not the New Testament accounts of Jesus and his reported resurrection are true, we need compelling historical evidence, something a mythology can't provide.

So, is there compelling evidence that Jesus was really the unique figure he is portrayed as in the New Testament? Several skeptics who initially agreed with Dawkins's assertion investigated the evidence for themselves. What did they discover? What evidence do we have that the eyewitness accounts are a clear picture of the one who changed our world?

In a criminal case, circumstantial evidence often provides sufficient clues for a verdict to be rendered. Yet for that to happen, clues from history must merge together like pieces in a puzzle. When we assemble the historical facts surrounding Jesus Christ, will they form a clear picture of who he really is? Will that picture affirm or negate the New Testament accounts of his deity and resurrection?

According to author and lecturer Ravi Zacharias, it is possible to link Jesus' words and his life to form a picture of truth. He writes, "This is precisely what makes Jesus so unique. The whole range of both His life and His teaching can be subjected to the test of truth. Each aspect of His teaching is a link in the greater whole. Each facet is like the face of a diamond, catching the light as it is gently turned."[13]

In this investigation, we will be looking at the evidence for the real Jesus Christ. As we examine the evidence available to us, we will hear from non-Christian historians such as Josephus and Tacitus from around the time of Christ, and we will hear from secular historians of modern times. We will also hear from both Jesus' enemies and his friends. Our goal will be to see if the pieces connect together to form a clear picture of Jesus of Nazareth.

Beyond that, we will examine Jesus' claims, because if Jesus is who he claimed to be, his message has profound implications for you and me. Jesus spoke of a meaning to life. And he claimed that it is only through him that we will discover our ultimate purpose.

Is Jesus Christ, in fact, the one who flung the galaxies into existence and yet in some mysterious way also invaded our planet as a man two thousand years ago?

Let's take a look.

Let's discover the real Jesus.

Part I

IS JESUS GOD?

Chapter 1

WAS JESUS MERELY A GREAT MAN?

H AVE YOU EVER met a man who is the center of attention wherever he goes? Some mysterious, indefinable characteristic sets him apart from all other men. Well, that's the way it was two thousand years ago with Jesus Christ. "The Jesus of the gospels, unlike the Jesus of religious sentimentalism, is both gentle and tough, witty and serious, stern and tenderhearted. The one thing the people who met him could not do was to stereotype him. He demolished all their labels and expectations, upset their attempts to pigeonhole him as a prophet, a wonder-worker, or a conventional rabbi."[1]

But it wasn't merely Jesus' personality that captivated those who heard him. Those who witnessed his words and life tell us that something about Jesus of Nazareth was different from all other men.

Jesus' only credentials were himself. He never wrote a book, commanded an army, held a political office, or owned property. He mostly traveled within a hundred miles of his village, attracting crowds who were amazed at his provocative words and stunning deeds.

While most great people eventually fade into history books, Jesus is still the focus of thousands of books and unparalleled media controversy. And much of that controversy revolves around the radical claims Jesus made about himself—claims that astounded both his followers and his adversaries.

It was primarily Jesus' unique claims that caused him to be viewed as a threat by the Roman authorities and the Jewish hierarchy. Although he was an outsider with no credentials or political power base, within three years, Jesus changed the world for the next twenty-plus centuries. Other moral and religious leaders have left an impact—but nothing like that itinerant preacher from Nazareth.

What was it about Jesus Christ that made the difference? Was he just a great man, or something more?

These questions get to the heart of who Jesus really was. Some believe he was merely a great moral teacher; others believe he was simply the leader of the world's greatest religion. But many believe something far more. Christians believe that in Jesus, God the Son actually visited us in human form. And they believe the evidence backs that up.[2] [See endnote 2.]

So, who is the *real* Jesus? As we take a deeper look at the world's most controversial person, we begin by asking, "Could Jesus have been merely a great moral teacher?"

Great Moral Teacher

Even those from other religions acknowledge that Jesus was a great moral teacher. Hindu leader Mahatma Gandhi, who was "mightily influenced by Jesus' teaching," spoke of Jesus as "a person who, in his love for the poor, oppressed, and outcast, stood against evil with his whole being to the end, despite the threat of violence."[3]

Likewise, Jewish scholar Joseph Klausner wrote, "It is universally admitted . . . that Christ taught the purest and sublimest ethics . . . which throws the moral precepts and maxims of the wisest men of antiquity far into the shade."[4]

Jesus' Sermon on the Mount has been called the most superlative teaching of human ethics ever uttered by an individual. In fact, much of what we know today as equal rights actually is the result of Jesus' teaching. Historian Will Durant, a non-Christian, said of Jesus that "he lived and struggled unremittingly for 'equal rights'; in modern times he would have been sent to Siberia. 'He that is greatest among you, let him be your servant'—this is the inversion of all political wisdom, of all sanity."[5]

Many, like Gandhi, have tried to separate Jesus' teaching on ethics from his claims about himself, believing that he was simply a great man who taught lofty moral principles. This was also the approach of one of America's Founding Fathers.

Thomas Jefferson cut and pasted a copy of the New Testament, removing sections he thought referred to Jesus' deity, while leaving in other passages regarding Jesus' ethical and moral teaching.[6] Jefferson carried around his cut-and-pasted New Testament with him, revering Jesus as perhaps the greatest moral teacher of all time, while denying his miracles.

In fact, Jefferson's memorable words in the Declaration of Independence were rooted in Jesus' teaching that each person is of immense and equal importance to God, regardless of sex, race, or social status. The famous document sets forth, "We hold these truths to be self-evident, that all men are created equal, that they are endowed by their Creator with certain unalienable Rights."

By simply cutting and pasting his revised New Testament, Jefferson never addressed the issue that if Jesus falsely claimed to be God, he couldn't have been a good moral teacher.

But did Jesus really claim deity? Before we look at what Jesus claimed, we need to examine the possibility that he was simply a great religious leader.

Great Religious Leader

Surprisingly, Jesus never claimed to be a religious leader. He never got into religious politics or pushed an ambitious agenda, and he ministered almost entirely outside the established religious framework.

When one compares Jesus with the other great religious leaders, a remarkable distinction emerges. Ravi Zacharias, who grew up in a Hindu culture, has studied world religions and observed a fundamental distinction between Jesus Christ and the founders of other major religions.

> In all of these, there emerges an instruction, a way of living. It is not Zoroaster to whom you turn; it is Zoroaster to whom you listen. It is not Buddha who delivers you; it is his Noble Truths that instruct you. It is not Mohammad who transforms you; it is the beauty of the Koran that woos you. By contrast, Jesus did not only teach or expound His message. He was identical with His message.[7]

The truth of Zacharias's point is underscored by the number of times in the Gospels that Jesus' teaching message was simply "Come to me" or "Follow me" or "Obey me." Jesus also made it clear that his primary mission was to forgive sins—something only God could do. Prior to Jesus, "the Temple represented everything that made Israel unique in the world. But Jesus changed all that. Forgiveness of sin was now found in him, not in the Temple cult. He claimed the authority to cancel the debt of sin and offer new life."[8] Former skeptic C. S. Lewis remarks of Jesus, "The things He says are very different from what any other teacher has said. Others say, 'This is the truth about the Universe. This is the way you ought to go.' But He says, 'No man can reach absolute reality, except through Me.'"[9]

In *The World's Great Religions*, Huston Smith observed, "Only two people ever astounded their contemporaries so much that the question they evoked was not 'Who is he?' but 'What is he?' They were Jesus and Buddha. The answers these two gave were exactly the opposite. Buddha said unequivocally that he was a mere man, not a god—almost as if he foresaw later attempts to worship him. Jesus, on the other hand, claimed . . . to be divine."[10]

And that leads us to the question of what Jesus really did claim for himself. Specifically, did Jesus claim to be God?

Chapter 2

DID JESUS CLAIM TO BE GOD?

M ANY SCHOLARS ARE convinced that Jesus claimed to be God. Although, as a man, Jesus honored his Father as God, there were many times when he made statements and claims that set him apart from all other men. Author John Piper, for instance, explains that Jesus claimed power uniquely belonging to God.

> Jesus' friends and enemies were staggered again and again by what he said and did. He would be walking down the road, seemingly like any other man, then turn and say something like, "Before Abraham was, I am." Or, "If you have seen me, you have seen the Father." Or, very calmly, after being accused of blasphemy, he would say, "The Son of Man has authority on earth to forgive sins." To the dead he might simply say, "Come

forth," or, "Rise up." And they would obey. To the storms on the sea he would say, "Be still." And to a loaf of bread he would say, "Become a thousand meals." And it was done immediately.[1]

But what did Jesus really mean by such statements and nature-defying deeds? Is it possible Jesus was merely a prophet like Moses or Elijah? Even a superficial reading of the Gospels reveals that Jesus claimed to be someone more than a prophet. No other prophet had made such claims about himself; in fact as we will see, no other prophet ever put himself in God's place as Jesus did.

Some argue that because Jesus never explicitly declared "I am God," he denied his own deity. They argue, "If Jesus didn't say those exact words, he must not be God." But how can anyone dictate to the creator of the universe what he must or must not say? Is it possible Jesus had another way of revealing his deity to us? To find out, we need to examine more closely how Jesus revealed himself to others.

For example, Jesus also never explicitly declared, "I am a prophet." Yet his followers considered him to be as much of a prophet as Moses and Elijah. Likewise, Jesus never stated verbatim, "I am the Messiah," but when asked, he acknowledged he was, and his disciples had no doubt that he was the fulfillment of numerous messianic prophecies.

DID JESUS CLAIM TO BE GOD?

So can we rule out Jesus' deity because he didn't declare, "I am God"? Using that logic, we would have to conclude that Jesus wasn't a prophet or the Messiah either. To discover the real Jesus, we must look further at the statements he made about himself in the context of his Jewish audience and how they would have perceived them.

In fact, Jesus' statements about himself contradict the notion that he was merely a great man or a prophet. On more than one occasion, Jesus referred to himself as God's Son. Biblical scholar Peter Kreeft indicates this term meant Jesus was claiming to have the exact same essence as God the Father.[2]

When asked whether he thought it far-fetched for Jesus to be the Son of God, Bono, the lead singer of U2, answered:

> No, it's not far-fetched to me. Look, the secular response to the Christ story always goes like this: He was a great prophet, obviously a very interesting guy, had a lot to say along the lines of other great prophets, be they Elijah, Muhammad, Buddha, or Confucius. But actually Christ doesn't allow you that. He doesn't let you off the hook. Christ says, "No." I'm not saying I'm a teacher, don't call me a teacher. I'm not saying I'm a prophet . . . . I'm saying I'm God incarnate. And people say: No, no, please, just be a prophet. A prophet we can take.[3]

Certainly not everyone agrees with Bono's view of Jesus. But as one reads the Gospels, it is difficult to contradict the singer's understanding that Jesus could not have been simply a great prophet. It is Jesus' stunning claims that set him apart.

Before we examine some of Jesus' claims, it is important to understand that he made them in the context of the Jewish belief in one God (monotheism). No faithful Jew would ever believe in more than one God. And Jesus believed in the one God, praying to his Father as "the only true God."[4]

But in the same prayer, Jesus spoke of having *always existed* with his Father. And when Philip asked Jesus to show them the Father, Jesus said, "Don't you know me, Philip, even after I have been among you such a long time? Anyone who has seen me has seen the Father."[5] So the question is, was Jesus claiming to be the Hebrew God who created the universe, or was Jesus himself part of God's creation?

THE GOD OF ABRAHAM AND MOSES

Jesus continually referred to himself in ways that confounded his listeners. As Piper notes, Jesus made the audacious statement "Before Abraham was born, I am!" He told Martha and others around her, "I am the resurrection and the life. He who believes in me will live, even though he dies." Likewise, Jesus would make statements like "I am the light of the world" and "I am the way and the truth and the life."[6] These and several other of his claims were preceded by the sacred words for God, "I AM" (*ego eimi*).[7] [See endnote 7.] What did Jesus mean by such statements? What is the significance of the term "I AM," and why did he continually use it?

Once again, we must go back to context. In the Hebrew Scriptures, when Moses asked God his name at the burning bush, God answered, "I AM." He was revealing to Moses that he (Yahweh) is the one and only God, who is outside of time and has always existed. Incredibly, Jesus was identifying himself with the very same holy words God used in describing his eternal existence to Moses. The question is, why?

Since the time of Moses, no practicing Jew would ever refer to himself or anyone else by "I AM." As a result, Jesus' "I AM" claims infuriated the Jewish leaders. One time, for example, some leaders explained to Jesus why they were trying to kill him, saying, "Because you, a mere man, claim to be God."[8]

Jesus' usage of God's name for himself angered the religious leaders. The point is that these Old Testament scholars knew exactly what he was saying—he was claiming to be God, the creator of the universe. How do we know? Because it is only this claim that would have brought the accusation of blasphemy. To read into the text that Jesus claimed to be God is clearly warranted, not simply by his words, but also by their reaction to those words. [For more on Jesus' claim to deity, see Y-Jesus.com/Evidence2.]

C. S. Lewis initially considered Jesus a myth. But this literary genius, who knew myths well, concluded that Jesus had to have been a real person. Furthermore, as Lewis investigated the evidence for Jesus, he became convinced that not only was Jesus real, but also he was unlike any man who had ever lived. Lewis writes, "Then comes the real shock. Among these Jews there suddenly turns up a man who goes about talking as if He was God. He claims to forgive sins. He says He always existed. He says He is coming to judge the world at the end of time."[9]

To Lewis, Jesus' claims were simply too radical and profound to have been made by an ordinary teacher or religious leader.

REALLY GOD

Some have argued that Jesus was only claiming to be part of God. But the idea that we are all part of God, and that within us is the seed of divinity, is simply not a possible meaning for Jesus' words and actions. In fact, Jesus continually reinforced the Old Testament teaching that there is only one God.

Jesus taught that he is God in the way the Jews understood God and in the way the

Hebrew Scriptures portrayed God, not in the way Hinduism, pantheism or the New Age movement understands God. Neither Jesus nor his audience had been weaned on *Star Wars*, and so when they spoke of God, they were not speaking of cosmic forces. There is simply no basis to redefine what Jesus meant by the concept of God.

Lewis explains:

> Now let us get this clear. Among Pantheists, like the Indians, anyone might say that he was a part of God, or one with God . . . . But this man, since He was a Jew, could not mean that kind of God. God, in their language, meant the Being outside the world who had made it and was infinitely different from anything else. And when you have grasped that, you will see that what this man said was, quite simply, the most shocking thing that has ever been uttered by human lips.[10]

Certainly there are those who accept Jesus as a great teacher, yet are unwilling to call him God. As a deist, Thomas Jefferson had no problem accepting Jesus' teachings on morals and ethics while denying his deity.[11] But as we've said (and will explore further), if Jesus was not who he claimed to be, then we must examine some other alternatives, none of which would make him a great moral teacher. Lewis argued, "I am trying here to prevent anyone from saying the really foolish thing that people often say about

Him: 'I'm ready to accept Jesus as a great moral teacher, but I don't accept his claim to be God.' That is the one thing we must not say."[12]

But there's another way of looking at it. What if Jesus was simply not being truthful about his own identity?

Chapter 3

COULD JESUS HAVE BEEN A DECEIVER OR SELF-DECEIVED?

A S WE HAVE seen, in his quest for truth, former skeptic C. S. Lewis knew that he could not have it both ways with the identity of Jesus. Either Jesus was who he claimed to be—God in the flesh—or his claims were false. And if they were false, Jesus could not be a great moral teacher. He would either be lying intentionally or he would be a lunatic with a God complex. We'll consider these last two possibilities in this chapter.

Even Jesus' harshest critics rarely have called him a liar. That label certainly doesn't seem to fit with Jesus' high moral and ethical teaching. How could anyone think that the most righteous man who ever lived lied about his identity? But, Lewis argues, if Jesus isn't who he claimed to be, we must consider the option that he was intentionally misleading everyone. We'll start there.

LYING TO OTHERS

One of the best-known and most influential political works of all time was written by Niccolò Machiavelli in 1532. In his classic, *The Prince*, Machiavelli exalts power, success, image, and efficiency above loyalty, faith, and honesty. According to Machiavelli (Machiavellian principle), lying is okay if it accomplishes a political end.

Could Jesus Christ have built his entire ministry upon a lie just to gain power, fame, or success? It would seem that, if he had lied, someone would have discovered it and exposed him. In fact, his Jewish opponents were constantly trying to expose Jesus as a fraud and liar. They would barrage him with questions in attempts to trip him up and make him contradict himself. Yet Jesus responded with remarkable consistency, never once being untruthful.

The question we must deal with is this: What could possibly motivate Jesus to live his entire life as a lie? He taught that God was opposed to lying and hypocrisy, so he wouldn't have been doing it to please his Father. He certainly wouldn't have lied for his followers' benefit, since all but one were martyred for not renouncing his Lordship. And so we are left with only two other explanations, each of which is problematic.

Personal Benefit

Many people have lied for personal gain. In fact, the motivation of most lies is some perceived benefit to oneself. What could Jesus have hoped to gain from lying about his identity? Power would be the most obvious answer. If people believed he was God, he would have tremendous power. (That is why many ancient leaders, such as the Caesars, claimed divine origin.)

However, the record shows that Jesus shunned all attempts to move himself in the direction of seated power, instead chastising those who abused such power and lived their lives pursuing it. In fact, Jesus continually reached out to those without power, demonstrating love and compassion.

It would seem that if power were Jesus' motivation, he would have avoided the cross at all costs. Having one's hands and feet nailed to a wooden cross strips a person of all power. Yet Jesus told his disciples that the cross was his destiny and mission. How would dying on a Roman cross bring him power?

Death, of course, brings all things into proper focus. And while many martyrs have died for a cause they believed in, few have been willing to die for a known lie. Certainly all hopes for Jesus' own personal gain would have ended on the cross. Yet, to his last breath, he would not relinquish his claim of being the unique Son of God, a title that refers to Jesus' deity.[1]

A Legacy

So, if Jesus was above lying for personal benefit, is it possible he made false claims about himself in order to leave a legacy? Certainly nothing in Jesus' life or words is consistent with him lying, even to create a legacy. Furthermore, the prospect of being beaten to a pulp and nailed to a cross would quickly dampen the enthusiasm of most would-be superstars.

Here is another haunting fact. If Jesus were to have simply dropped the claim of being God's Son, he never would have been condemned. It was his claim to deity and his unwillingness to recant that got him crucified.

If enhancing his credibility and historical reputation was what motivated Jesus to lie, one must explain how a carpenter's son from a poor Galilean village could ever anticipate the events that would catapult his name to worldwide prominence. How would he know his message would survive? Jesus' disciples had fled and Peter had denied him. Not exactly the formula for launching a religious legacy.

Do historians believe Jesus lied? Scholars from the past twenty centuries have scrutinized Jesus' words and life to see if there is any evidence of a defect in his moral character. None have discovered any imperfection in him. In fact, even the most ardent skeptics are stunned by Jesus' moral and ethical purity.

COULD JESUS HAVE BEEN
A DECEIVER OR SELF-DECEIVED?

According to historian Philip Schaff, there is no evidence, either in church history or in secular history, that Jesus lied about anything. Schaff argued, "How, in the name of logic, common sense, and experience, could a deceitful, selfish, depraved man have invented, and consistently maintained from the beginning to end, the purest and noblest character known in history with the most perfect air of truth and reality?"[2]

To go with the option of liar seems to swim upstream against everything Jesus taught, lived, and died for. To most scholars, it just doesn't make sense. Yet, to deny Jesus' claims, one must come up with some explanation. And if Jesus' claims are not true, and he wasn't lying, the only option remaining is that he must have been self-deceived.

LYING TO HIMSELF

Albert Schweitzer, who was awarded the Nobel Prize in 1952 for his humanitarian efforts, had his own views about Jesus. Schweitzer, a non-Christian, concluded that insanity was behind Jesus' claim to be God. In other words, he believed Jesus was wrong about his claims but didn't intentionally lie. According to Schweitzer's theory, Jesus was deluded into actually believing he was the Messiah.

In his search for the real Jesus, C. S. Lewis considered this option carefully. He deduced that if Jesus' claims weren't true, then he must have been insane. Lewis reasoned that someone who claimed to be God would not be a great moral teacher. "He would either be a lunatic—on a level with the man who says he is a poached egg—or else he would be the Devil of Hell."[3]

Most who have studied Jesus' life and words acknowledge him as extremely rational and psychologically well balanced. Renowned French philosopher Jean-Jacques Rousseau (1712–1778), although his own life was filled with immorality and personal skepticism, acknowledged Jesus' superior character and presence of mind, stating, "When Plato describes his imaginary righteous man . . . he describes exactly the character of Christ . . . . If the life and death of Socrates are those of a philosopher, the life and death of Jesus Christ are those of a God."[4]

Not afraid to speak his mind, Bono continues his thoughts about Jesus by stating that a "nutcase" was the last thing one could label him. He argues, "So what you're left with is either Christ was who He said He was—or a complete nutcase. I mean, we're talking nutcase on the level of Charles Manson . . . . I'm not joking here. The idea that the entire course of civilization for over half of the globe could have its fate changed and turned upside down by a nutcase, for me that's far-fetched."[5]

LIAR, LUNATIC, OR LORD

So, was Jesus a liar or a lunatic, or was he the Son of God? The claims of Jesus Christ force us to choose. C. S. Lewis asks, "What are we to make of Jesus Christ?"[6] "The real question," according to Lewis, "is not what are we to make of Christ, but what is He to make of us?"[7] True to his words, Lewis allowed Jesus Christ to change his life. The former atheist then challenges us to make up our own minds about Jesus, stating:

> You must make your choice. Either this man was, and is, the Son of God: or else a madman or something worse. You can shut Him up for a fool, you can spit at Him and kill him as a demon or you can fall at his feet and call Him Lord and God. But let us not come with any patronizing nonsense about His being a great human teacher. He has not left that open to us. He did not intend to.[8]

In *Mere Christianity*, Lewis explores the options regarding the identity of Jesus, concluding that he is exactly who he claimed to be: the Son of God. His careful examination of the life and words of Jesus led this literary genius to renounce his former atheism and become a committed Christian.

Who Is the Real Jesus?

The greatest question in human history is "Who is the *real* Jesus Christ?" Bono, Lewis, and countless others have concluded that God the Son visited our planet in human form. But if that is true, then we would expect him to be alive today. And that is exactly what his followers believe.

The writers of the New Testament unanimously state that Jesus conquered death after being crucified and buried. But our secular world requires proof, and many have had difficulty believing such a feat possible. In the following chapters we will examine the evidence for the most astounding claim in history: that Jesus Christ rose bodily from a tomb three days after his crucifixion and death.

Part 2

DID JESUS RISE FROM THE DEAD?

Chapter 4

HOW WAS JESUS'
DEATH DIFFERENT
FROM OTHERS?

W^{E ALL WONDER} what will happen to us
after we die. When a loved one dies, we
long to see him or her again after our turn comes.
Will we have a glorious reunion with those we
love, or is death the end of all consciousness?

Jesus taught that life does not end after our
bodies die. He made this startling claim: "I am
the resurrection and the life. He who believes in
me will live, even though he dies."[1] According
to the eyewitnesses closest to him, Jesus then
demonstrated his power over death by rising
from the dead after being crucified and buried
for three days. It is this belief that has given hope
to Christians for nearly two thousand years.

But some people have no hope of life after
death. The atheistic philosopher Bertrand Russell
wrote, "I believe that when I die I shall rot, and

nothing of my own ego will survive."[2] Russell obviously didn't believe Jesus' words.

Jesus' followers wrote that he appeared alive to them after his crucifixion and burial. They claim not only to have seen him but also to have eaten with him, touched him, and spent forty days with him.

So, could this have been simply a story that grew over time, or is it based upon solid evidence? The answer to this question is foundational to Christianity. For if Jesus did rise from the dead, it would validate everything he said about himself, about the meaning of life, and about our destiny after death.

If Jesus did rise from the dead, then he alone would have the answers to what life is about and what is facing us after we die. On the other hand, if the resurrection account of Jesus is not true, then Christianity would be founded upon a lie. Theologian R. C. Sproul puts it this way: "The claim of resurrection is vital to Christianity. If Christ has been raised from the dead by God, then He has the credentials and certification that no other religious leader possesses. Buddha is dead. Mohammad is dead. Moses is dead. Confucius is dead. But, according to . . . Christianity, Christ is alive."[3]

Many skeptics have attempted to disprove the resurrection. Josh McDowell was one such skeptic who spent more than seven hundred hours researching the evidence for the resurrection.

McDowell stated this regarding the importance of the resurrection: "I have come to the conclusion that the resurrection of Jesus Christ is one of the most wicked, vicious, heartless hoaxes ever foisted upon the minds of men, OR it is the most fantastic fact of history."[4] McDowell wrote his classic work, *The New Evidence That Demands A Verdict*, documenting what the evidence reveals about Jesus' resurrection.

So, is Jesus' resurrection a fantastic fact or a vicious hoax? To find out, we need to look at the evidence of history and draw our own conclusions. Let's see what skeptics who investigated the resurrection discovered for themselves.

Cynics and Skeptics

Sadly, not everyone is willing to fairly examine the evidence. Russell admits he was "not concerned" with historical facts regarding Jesus. Historian Joseph Campbell, without citing evidence, calmly told his PBS television audience that the resurrection of Jesus is not a factual event. Other scholars, such as John Dominic Crossan of the Jesus Seminar, agree with him. None of these cynics present any evidence for their views.[5]

True skeptics, as opposed to cynics, are interested in evidence. In a *Skeptic* magazine editorial entitled "What Is a Skeptic?" the following definition is given: "Skepticism is . . . the application of reason to any and all ideas—no sacred cows allowed. In other words . . . skeptics do not go into an investigation closed to the possibility that a phenomenon might be real or that a claim might be true. When we say we are 'skeptical,' we mean that we must see compelling evidence before we believe."[6]

Unlike Russell and Crossan, many true skeptics have investigated the evidence for Jesus' resurrection. We will hear from some of them and see how they analyzed the evidence for what is perhaps the most important question in the history of the human race: Did Jesus really rise from the dead?

SELF-PROPHECY

In advance of his death, Jesus told his disciples that he would be betrayed, arrested, and crucified and that he would come back to life three days later. That's a strange plan! What was behind it? Jesus was no entertainer willing to perform for others on demand. Instead, he promised that his death and resurrection would prove to people (if their minds and hearts were open) that he was indeed the Messiah.

Bible scholar Wilbur Smith remarked about Jesus, "When He said that He himself would rise again from the dead, the third day after He was crucified, He said something that only a fool would dare say, if He expected longer the devotion of any disciples—unless He was sure

He was going to rise. No founder of any world religion known to men ever dared say a thing like that."[7]

In other words, since Jesus had clearly told his disciples that he would rise again after his death, failure to keep that promise would expose him as a fraud. But we're getting ahead of ourselves. How did Jesus die (if he really did die) before the news began spreading that he rose again?

A HORRIFIC DEATH AND THEN . . . ?

You know what Jesus' last hours of earthly life were like if you watched the movie by road warrior/brave heart Mel Gibson. If you missed parts of *The Passion of the Christ* because you were shielding your eyes (it would have been easier to simply shoot the movie with a red filter on the camera), just flip to the back pages of any Gospel in your New Testament to find out what you missed.

As Jesus predicted, he was betrayed by one of his own disciples, Judas Iscariot, and was arrested. In a sham trial under the Roman governor Pontius Pilate, he was convicted of treason and condemned to die on a wooden cross. Prior to being nailed to the cross, Jesus was brutally beaten with a Roman cat-o'-nine-tails, a whip with bits of bone and metal that would rip flesh. He was punched repeatedly, kicked, and spat upon.

Then, using mallets, the Roman executioners pounded the heavy wrought-iron nails into Jesus' hands and feet. Finally, they dropped the cross in a hole in the ground between two other crosses bearing convicted thieves.

Jesus hung there in agony for approximately six hours. Then, at 3:00 in the afternoon—that is, at exactly the same time the Passover lamb was being sacrificed as a sin offering (a little symbolism there, you think?)—Jesus cried out, "It is finished" (in Aramaic), and died.[8] Suddenly the sky went dark and an earthquake shook the land, tearing the Temple veil that separated the Holy of Holies from the people. This New Testament account of darkness was confirmed as historical by a contemporary pagan source.[9] [See endnote 9.]

An even greater darkness of depression annihilated the dreams of those who had become inspired by his charisma and joyful vitality. Former Chancellor of Britain, Lord Hailsham, writes, "The tragedy of the Cross was not that they crucified a melancholy figure, full of moral precepts, ascetic and gloomy . . . . What they crucified was a young man, vital, full of life and the joy of it, the Lord of life itself . . . someone so utterly attractive that people followed him for the sheer fun of it."[10]

Pilate wanted verification that Jesus was dead before allowing his crucified body to be buried. So a Roman guard thrust a spear into

Jesus' side. The mixture of blood and water that flowed out was a clear indication that Jesus was dead. "The dead do not bleed, ordinarily, but the right auricle of the human heart holds liquid blood after death, and the outer sac holds a serum called hydropericardium."[11] Once his death was positively confirmed by the guards, Jesus' body was then taken down from the cross and buried in Joseph of Arimathea's tomb. Roman guards next sealed the tomb and secured it with a twenty-four-hour watch.

Meanwhile, Jesus' disciples were in shock. Dr. J. P. Moreland explains how devastated and confused they were after Jesus' death on the cross. "They no longer had confidence that Jesus had been sent by God. They also had been taught that God would not let his Messiah suffer death. So they dispersed. The Jesus movement was all but stopped in its tracks."[12]

All hope was vanquished. Rome and the Jewish leaders had prevailed—or so it seemed.

But it wasn't the end. The Jesus movement surprisingly did not disappear, and in fact Christianity exists today as the world's largest religion. In order to understand why, we've got to know what happened after Jesus' body was taken down from the cross and laid in the tomb.

Chapter 5

CAN WE
EXPLAIN AWAY
THE RESURRECTION?

I N A *NEW York Times* article, Peter Steinfels cites the startling events that occurred three days after Jesus' death. "Shortly after Jesus was executed, his followers were suddenly galvanized from a baffled and cowering group into people whose message about a living Jesus and a coming kingdom, preached at the risk of their lives, eventually changed an empire. Something happened . . . . But exactly what?"[1] That's the question we have to answer with an investigation into the facts.

There are only five plausible explanations for Jesus' alleged resurrection, as portrayed in the New Testament:

1. Jesus didn't really die on the cross.
2. The "resurrection" was a conspiracy.

3. The disciples were hallucinating.
4. The account is legendary.
5. It really happened.

Let's work our way through these options and see which one best fits the facts. We'll consider the first four options in this chapter and the fifth in the next.

SIGNING THE DEATH CERTIFICATE

"Marley was deader than a doornail, of that there was no doubt." So begins Charles Dickens's *A Christmas Carol*, the author not wanting anyone to be mistaken as to the supernatural character of what is soon to take place. In the same way, before we take on the role of CSI (crime scene investigator) and piece together evidence for a resurrection, we must first establish that there was, in fact, a corpse. After all, occasionally the newspapers will report on some "corpse" in a morgue who was found stirring and recovered. Could something like that have happened with Jesus?

Some have proposed that Jesus lived through the crucifixion and was revived by the cool, damp air in the tomb. But that theory doesn't square with the medical evidence. An article in the *Journal of the American Medical Association* explains why this so-called "swoon theory" is untenable. "Clearly, the weight of historical and medical evidence indicated that Jesus was dead . . . . The spear, thrust between His right ribs, probably perforated not only the right lung, but also the pericardium and heart and thereby ensured His death."[2] But skepticism of this verdict may be in order, as this case has been cold for two thousand years. At the very least, we need a second opinion.

One place to find that is in the reports of non-Christian historians from around the time when Jesus lived. Three of these historians mentioned the death of Jesus.

- Lucian (c. 120–after 180) referred to Jesus as a "crucified sophist," or philosopher.[3]
- Josephus (c. 37–c. 100) wrote, "At this time there appeared Jesus, a wise man, for he was a doer of amazing deeds. When Pilate condemned him to the cross, the leading men among us, having accused him, those who loved him did not cease to do so."[4] [See endnote 4.]
- Tacitus (c. 56–c. 120) wrote, "Christus, from whom the name had its origin, suffered the extreme penalty . . . at the hands of our procurator, Pontius Pilate."[5]

This is a bit like going into the archives and finding that on one spring day in the first century, *The Jerusalem Post* ran a front-page story saying that Jesus was crucified and dead. Not bad detective work, and fairly conclusive.

In fact, there is no historical account from Christians, Romans, or Jews that disputes either Jesus' death or his burial. If Jesus hadn't really died on the cross, one wonders why his enemies wouldn't have shouted it from their rooftops, as his followers publicly proclaimed his crucifixion and resurrection.

Even Crossan, a skeptic of the resurrection, agrees that Jesus really lived and died on the cross. He states, "That he was crucified is as sure as anything historical can ever be."[6] In light of such historical and medical evidence, we seem to be on good grounds for dismissing the first of our five options. Jesus was clearly dead. "Of that there was no doubt."

THE MATTER OF AN EMPTY TOMB

No serious historian really doubts Jesus was dead when he was taken down from the cross. However, many have questioned how Jesus' body disappeared from the tomb. Some have proposed that a plot was devised to make it look like Jesus had risen.

English journalist Dr. Frank Morison initially thought the resurrection was either a myth or a hoax, and he began research to write a book refuting it.[7] The book became famous—but for reasons other than its original intent.

Morison began by attempting to solve the case of the empty tomb. The tomb belonged to a member of the Sanhedrin council, Joseph of Arimathea. In

Israel at that time, to be on the council was to be a rock star. Everyone knew who was on the council. Joseph must have been a real person. Otherwise, the Jewish leaders would have exposed the story as a fraud in their attempt to disprove the resurrection. Also, Joseph's tomb would have been at a well-known location and easily identifiable, so any thoughts of Jesus being "lost in the graveyard" would need to be dismissed.

Morison wondered why Jesus' enemies would have allowed the "empty tomb myth" to persist if it weren't true. The discovery of Jesus' body would have instantly killed the entire plot.

And what is known historically of Jesus' enemies is that they accused Jesus' disciples of stealing the body, an accusation clearly predicated on a shared belief that the tomb was empty.

Dr. Paul L. Maier, professor of ancient history at Western Michigan University, similarly stated, "If all the evidence is weighed carefully and fairly, it is indeed justifiable . . . to conclude that the tomb in which Jesus was buried was actually empty on the morning of the first Easter. And no shred of evidence has yet been discovered . . . that would disprove this statement."[8]

The Jewish leaders were stunned. They accused the disciples of stealing Jesus' body. But the Romans had assigned a twenty-four-hour watch at the tomb with a trained guard unit (from four to sixteen soldiers). Josh McDowell notes that these were not ordinary soldiers. "When that guard unit failed in its duty—if they fell asleep, left their position, or failed in any way—there are a number of historical sources that go back and describe what happens. Many of them are stripped of their own clothes, they are burned alive in a fire started with their own garments or they are crucified upside down. The Roman Guard unit was committed to discipline and they feared failure in any way."[9]

It would have been impossible for anyone to have slipped by these trained professionals and to have moved a two-ton stone. Yet the stone was moved away and the body of Jesus was missing.

If Jesus' body were anywhere to be found, his enemies would have quickly exposed the resurrection as a fraud. Tom Anderson, former president of the California Trial Lawyers Association, summarizes the strength of this argument. "With an event so well publicized, don't you think that it's reasonable that one historian, one eyewitness, one antagonist would record for all time that he had seen Christ's body? . . . The silence of history is deafening when it comes to the testimony against the resurrection."[10]

So, with a known tomb clearly empty, Morison accepted the evidence as solid that Jesus' body had somehow disappeared from the tomb.

Can We Explain Away the Resurrection?

Grave Robbing

Morison still had doubts about what caused the tomb to be empty. An empty tomb is insufficient proof that Jesus had risen. As the skeptical journalist continued his investigation, he began to examine the motives of Jesus' followers. Maybe the supposed resurrection was actually a stolen body. But if so, how does one account for all the reported appearances of a resurrected Jesus? Historian Paul Johnson, in *History of the Jews,* wrote, "What mattered was not the circumstances of his death but the fact that he was widely and obstinately believed, by an expanding circle of people, to have risen again."[11]

The tomb was indeed empty. But it wasn't the mere absence of a body that could have galvanized Jesus' followers (especially if they had been the ones who had stolen it). Something extraordinary must have happened, for the followers of Jesus ceased mourning, ceased hiding, and began fearlessly proclaiming that they had seen Jesus alive.

Each eyewitness account reports that Jesus suddenly appeared bodily to his followers, the women first. Morison wondered why conspirators would make women central to its plot. In the first century, women had virtually no rights or status. If the plot were to succeed, Morison reasoned, the conspirators would have portrayed men, not women, as the first to see Jesus alive. And yet we hear that women touched him, spoke with him, and were the first to find the empty tomb.

Later, according to the eyewitness accounts, all the disciples saw Jesus on more than ten separate occasions. They wrote that he showed them his hands and feet and told them to touch him. And he reportedly ate with them and later appeared alive to more than five hundred followers on one occasion.

Legal scholar John Warwick Montgomery stated, "In 56 AD the Apostle Paul wrote that over 500 people had seen the risen Jesus and that most of them were still alive (1 Corinthians 15:6ff.). It passes the bounds of credibility that the early Christians could have manufactured such a tale and then preached it among those who might easily have refuted it simply by producing the body of Jesus."[12]

Bible scholars Geisler and Turek agree. "If the Resurrection had not occurred, why would the Apostle Paul give such a list of supposed eyewitnesses? He would immediately lose all credibility with his Corinthian readers by lying so blatantly."[13]

The apostle Peter told a crowd in Caesarea why he and the other disciples were so convinced Jesus was alive. "We apostles are witnesses of all he did throughout Israel and in Jerusalem. They put him to death by crucifying him, but God raised him to life three days later . . . . We were those who ate and drank with him after he rose from the dead."[14]

British Bible scholar Michael Green remarked, "The appearances of Jesus are as well authenticated as anything in antiquity . . . . There can be no rational doubt that they occurred."[15]

Consistent to the End

As if the eyewitness reports were not enough to challenge Morison's skepticism, he was also baffled by the disciples' behavior. A fact of history that has stumped historians, psychologists, and skeptics alike is that these eleven former cowards were suddenly willing to suffer humiliation, torture, and death. All but one of Jesus' disciples were slain as martyrs. Would they have done so much for a lie, knowing they had taken the body?

The Islamic suicide terrorists on September 11, 2001, proved that some will die for a false cause they believe in. Yet to be a willing martyr for a known lie is insanity. As Paul Little wrote, "Men will die for what they believe to be true, though it may actually be false. They do not, however, die for what they know is a lie."[16] Jesus' disciples behaved in a manner consistent with a genuine belief that their leader was alive.

No one has adequately explained why the disciples would have been willing to die for a known lie. But even if they all conspired to lie about Jesus' resurrection, how could they have kept the conspiracy going for decades without at least one of them selling out for money or position? J. P. Moreland wrote, "Those who lie for personal gain do not stick together very long, especially when hardship decreases the benefits."[17]

Chuck Colson, implicated in the Watergate scandal during President Nixon's administration, pointed out the difficulty of several people maintaining a lie for an extended period of time.

> I know the resurrection is a fact, and Watergate proved it to me. How? Because 12 men testified they had seen Jesus raised from the dead, and then they proclaimed that truth for 40 years, never once denying it. Every one was beaten, tortured, stoned and put in prison. They would not have endured that if it weren't true. Watergate embroiled 12 of the most powerful men in the world—and they couldn't keep a lie for three weeks. You're telling me 12 apostles could keep a lie for 40 years? Absolutely impossible.[18]

Something happened that changed everything for these men and women. Morison acknowledged, "Whoever comes to this problem has sooner or later to confront a fact that cannot be explained away . . . . This fact is that . . . a profound conviction came to the little group of people—a change that attests to the fact that Jesus had risen from the grave."[19] We have to move on to the third option: hallucination.

Can We Explain Away the Resurrection?

Seeing Things

People still think they see a fat, gray-haired Elvis darting into Dunkin' Donuts®. And then there are those who believe they spent last night with aliens in the mother ship being subjected to unspeakable testing. Sometimes certain people can "see" things they want to, things that aren't really there. And that's why some have claimed that the disciples were so distraught over the crucifixion that their desire to see Jesus alive caused mass hallucination. Plausible?

Psychologist Gary Collins, former president of the American Association of Christian Counselors, was asked about the possibility that hallucinations were behind the disciples' radically changed behavior. Collins remarked, "Hallucinations are individual occurrences. By their very nature, only one person can see a given hallucination at a time. They certainly aren't something which can be seen by a group of people."[20]

Hallucination is not even a remote possibility, according to psychologist Thomas J. Thorburn. "It is absolutely inconceivable that . . . five hundred persons, of average soundness of mind . . . should experience all kinds of sensuous impressions—visual, auditory, tactual—and that all these . . . experiences should rest entirely upon . . . hallucination."[21]

Furthermore, in the psychology of hallucinations, people would need to be in a frame of mind where they so wished to see that person that their mind contrives it. Two major leaders of the early church, James and Paul, both encountered a resurrected Jesus, neither expecting nor hoping for the pleasure. James was skeptical of Jesus' deity prior to the resurrection. The apostle Paul, in fact, led the earliest persecutions of Christians, and his conversion remains inexplicable except for his own testimony that Jesus appeared to him, resurrected.

The hallucination theory, then, appears to be another dead end. What else could explain away the resurrection?

FROM LIE TO LEGEND

Some unconvinced skeptics attribute the resurrection story to a legend that began with one or more persons lying or thinking they saw the resurrected Jesus. Over time, the legend would have grown and been embellished as it was passed around.

On the surface this seems like a plausible scenario. But there are three major problems with that theory.

First, legends rarely develop while multiple eyewitnesses are alive to refute them. One historian of ancient Rome and Greece, A. N. Sherwin-White, argued that the resurrection news spread too soon and too quickly for it to have been a legend.[22]

Second, legends usually develop over several centuries by oral tradition and don't come with contemporary historical documents that can be verified. Yet the Gospels were written within three decades of the resurrection.[23] Paul's historical account of the resurrection, written a decade earlier, cites a creed many critical scholars say originated "within five years of Jesus' crucifixion and from the disciples themselves."[24]

Third, the legend theory doesn't adequately explain the fact of the empty tomb, the Jews' argument that the body was stolen, or the historically verified conviction of the apostles that Jesus was alive.[25]

The perspective that the resurrection was a legend doesn't seem to hold up any better than the other attempts to explain away this amazing claim. It seems that Jesus really was dead, that the disciples showed no sign of engaging in a conspiracy to promote a false resurrection, that they knew what they were talking about when they said they saw the risen Jesus, and that the resurrection could not have been a legend that grew up over time.

That leaves us with one extraordinary conclusion.

Chapter 6

WHAT IF
THE RESURRECTION
REALLY HAPPENED?

JOURNALIST FRANK MORISON was bewildered by the fact that "a tiny insignificant movement was able to prevail over the cunning grip of the Jewish establishment, as well as the might of Rome."

Morison further wrote, "Within twenty years, the claim of these Galilean peasants had disrupted the Jewish church . . . . In less than fifty years it had begun to threaten the peace of the Roman Empire. When we have said everything that can be said . . . we stand confronted with the greatest mystery of all. Why did it win?"[1]

By all rights, if there were no resurrection, Christianity should have died out at the cross when the disciples fled for their lives. But instead the apostles went on to establish a growing Christian movement.

J.N.D. Anderson wrote, "Think of the psychological absurdity of picturing a little band of defeated cowards cowering in an upper room one day and a few days later transformed into a company that no persecution could silence—and then attempting to attribute this dramatic change to nothing more convincing than a miserable fabrication . . . . That simply wouldn't make sense."[2]

The story of the resurrection, as astounding as it is, sounds more and more plausible. Or so it seemed to Morison.

A SURPRISE CONCLUSION

With myth, hallucination, and a flawed autopsy ruled out, with incontrovertible evidence for an empty tomb, with a substantial body of eyewitnesses to his reappearance, and with the inexplicable transformation and impact upon the world of those who claimed to have seen him, Morison became convinced that his preconceived bias against Jesus Christ's resurrection had been wrong. He began writing a different book—entitled *Who Moved the Stone?*—to detail his new conclusions. Morison simply followed the trail of evidence, clue by clue, until the truth of the case seemed clear to him. His surprise was that the evidence led to a belief in the resurrection.

In his first chapter, "The Book that Refused to Be Written," this former skeptic explained

how the evidence convinced him that Jesus'
resurrection was an actual historical event. "It
was as though a man set out to cross a forest by
a familiar and well-beaten track and came out
suddenly where he did not expect to come out."[3]

Morison is not alone. Countless other skeptics
have examined the evidence for Jesus' resurrection and accepted it as the most astounding fact
in all of human history. C. S. Lewis, who once
had even doubted Jesus' existence, was also
persuaded by the evidence for Jesus' resurrection. He writes:

"Something perfectly new in the history of
the Universe had happened. Christ had defeated
death. The door which had always been locked
had for the very first time been forced open."[4]

Let's consider just one more skeptic who was
persuaded by the evidence.

A STUNNED PROFESSOR

One of those who originally thought the resurrection was simply a myth, only to reverse his
position like Morison, was one of the world's
leading legal scholars, Dr. Simon Greenleaf.
Greenleaf helped to put the Harvard Law School
on the map. He wrote the three-volume legal
masterpiece, *A Treatise on the Law of Evidence*,
which has been called the "greatest single authority in the entire literature of legal procedure."[5]

The U.S. judicial system today still relies on rules of evidence established by Greenleaf.

While teaching law at Harvard, Professor Greenleaf stated to his class that the resurrection of Jesus Christ was simply a legend. As an atheist, he thought miracles to be impossible. In a rebuttal, three of his law students challenged him to apply his acclaimed rules of evidence to the resurrection account.

After much prodding, Greenleaf accepted his students' challenge and began an investigation into the evidence. Focusing his brilliant legal mind on the facts of history, Greenleaf attempted to prove the resurrection account was false.

Yet the more Greenleaf investigated the record of history, the more stunned he was at the powerful evidence supporting the claim that Jesus had indeed risen from the tomb. Greenleaf's skepticism was being challenged by an event that had changed the course of human history.

Greenleaf was unable to explain several dramatic changes that took place shortly after Jesus died, the most baffling being the behavior of the disciples. It wasn't just one or two disciples who insisted Jesus had risen; it was all of them. Applying his own rules of evidence to the facts, Greenleaf arrived at his verdict.

In a shocking reversal of his position, Greenleaf accepted Jesus' resurrection as the best explanation for the events that took place immediately after his crucifixion. To this brilliant legal scholar and former atheist, it would have been impossible for the disciples to persist with their conviction that Jesus had risen if they hadn't actually seen the risen Christ.[6]

In his book *The Testimony of the Evangelists,* Greenleaf documents the evidence that caused him to change his mind. In his conclusion he challenges those who seek the truth about the resurrection to fairly examine the evidence.

Greenleaf was so persuaded by the evidence that he renounced his atheism and became a committed Christian. He believed that any unbiased person who honestly examines the evidence as in a court of law will conclude what he did—that Jesus Christ has truly risen.[7]

But some may wonder, "What does the fact that Jesus defeated death have to do with my life?" The answer to that question is what New Testament Christianity is all about; Jesus told us that it has everything to do with us and our eternal future.

In the following chapters we will look at what Jesus said about God, about himself, and about us—and therefore why his resurrection is so vitally important.

Part 3

IS JESUS RELEVANT TODAY?

Chapter 7

WHAT DID JESUS SAY ABOUT GOD?

WHEN FORMER SKEPTIC Josh McDowell was a college student, he thought Jesus was just another religious leader who set up impossible rules to live by. He considered him to be totally irrelevant to his life, not wanting any part of Jesus or his followers.

Then one day, at a student union lunch table, McDowell sat next to a coed with a radiant smile. Intrigued, he asked her why she was so happy. Her immediate reply was "Jesus Christ!"

Jesus Christ? McDowell bristled, firing back, "Oh, for God's sake, don't give me that garbage. I'm fed up with religion. I'm fed up with the church. I'm fed up with the Bible. Don't give me that garbage about religion."

But the unfazed student calmly informed him, "Mister, I didn't say religion. I said Jesus Christ."[1]

McDowell was stunned. He didn't want any part of religious hypocrisy. Yet here was this joyful Christian woman talking about Jesus as someone who had brought meaning to her life.

Jesus Christ claimed to answer the deep, perplexing questions about our existence. At one time or another, we all question what life is all about. Have you ever watched an eagle soar or gazed up at the stars on a pitch-black evening and wondered about the mystery of life? Or have you ever watched the shimmering sun set into the blue ocean water and thought about life's biggest questions?

- "Who am I?"
- "Why am I here?"
- "Where am I going after I die?"

If Jesus actually defeated death, as the evidence suggests, then he alone would be able to tell us what life is all about and answer the question "Where am I going?" He would be able to establish our identities, give us meaning in life, and provide hope for the future.

Therefore, we need to look at the things he said about what really matters. Let's start with three key points he made about God.

GOD IS RELATIONAL

Many think of God more as a force than a person we can know and enjoy. The God of whom

Jesus spoke is not like the impersonal Force in *Star Wars*, whose goodness is measured in voltage. Neither did Jesus refer to him as some unsympathetic bogeyman in the sky, delighting in making our lives miserable.

On the contrary, according to Jesus, God is relational like us, but much more so. He thinks. He hears. He communicates in language we can understand. Jesus told us and showed us what God is like. According to Jesus, God knows each of us intimately and personally and desires our companionship. He also knows our needs, even before we ask him.[2]

God Is Loving

And Jesus told us that God is loving. Jesus demonstrated God's love wherever he went, as he healed the sick and reached out to the hurting and poor.

Jesus taught that God's love is radically different from ours in that it is not based upon attraction or performance. It is totally sacrificial and unselfish. Jesus compared God's love with the love of a perfect father. A good father wants the best for his children, sacrifices for them, and provides for them. He is even willing to give his life for them. But in their best interests, he also disciplines them.

Jesus illustrates God's heart of love with a story about a rebellious son who rejected his father's advice about life and what is important.[3]

Arrogant and self-willed, the son wanted to quit working for his father, leave home, and "live it up." Rather than waiting until his father was ready to give him his inheritance, he began insisting that his father give it to him early.

In Jesus' story, the father granted his son's request. At first the son was elated at his freedom to do what he wanted. But things went badly for the son. After squandering his money on self-indulgence, the rebellious son had to go to work on a pig farm. Soon he was so hungry that even the pig feed looked good. Despondent and not sure his father would accept him back, he packed his bag and headed home.

Jesus tells us that not only did his father welcome him home, but he actually ran out to meet him. He hadn't forgotten his son, but had been patiently waiting for him to return. And then the father went totally radical with his love, dressing the son with his finest robe, after which he threw a huge party celebrating his return. It was a time of great joy.

It is interesting that even though the father greatly loved his son, he didn't chase after him and try to coax him to return home. He let the son he loved feel pain and suffer the consequences of his rebellious choices. In a similar way, the Scriptures teach that God's love will never compromise what is best for us. It will allow us to suffer the consequences of our own wrong choices, so we will recognize our need of him.

Jesus also taught that God will never compromise his character. Character is who we are down deep. It is our essence, from which all our thoughts and actions stem. So, what is God like—down deep?

GOD IS HOLY

Throughout the Scriptures (nearly six hundred times), God is spoken of as "holy." During his high priestly prayer, for example, Jesus reverently addresses his Father as "holy Father."[4] *Holy* means that God's character is morally pure and perfect in every way. Unblemished. This means that he never entertains a thought that is impure or inconsistent with his moral excellence.

Furthermore, God's holiness means that evil cannot exist in his presence. Since evil is the opposite of his nature, he hates it. It's like pollution to him. God will not permit the pure water of his holiness to be polluted by the polluted stream of our sin. Although God loves us, his opposition to sin is also part of his holy character. J. I. Packer writes that God's hatred against sin is "a right and necessary reaction to objective moral evil . . . . God's wrath is always judicial."[5]

But if God is holy and abhors evil, why didn't he make our character like his? Why are there child molesters, murderers, rapists, and perverts? And why do we struggle so with our own moral choices? That brings us to the next part of our quest for meaning. What did Jesus say about us?

Chapter 8

WHAT DID JESUS SAY ABOUT US?

ALTHOUGH OTHER PHILOSOPHERS and religious leaders have offered their answers to the meaning of life, only Jesus Christ proved his credentials by rising from the dead. As we have seen, many who originally scoffed at Jesus' resurrection have discovered compelling evidence that it really occurred.

And if Jesus truly rose from the dead, he is alive today. Furthermore, his promises to us can be counted on. Jesus offers life with real meaning, not just in this world, but also in the one to come. He said that life is about much more than making money, having fun, being successful, and then ending up in a graveyard. Yet many people still try to find meaning in fame and success.

World-famous entertainer Madonna attempted to answer the question, "Why am I here?" by becoming a diva. She confessed, "There were many years when I thought fame, fortune, and public approval would bring me happiness. But one day you wake up and realize they don't. . . . I still felt something was missing . . . . I wanted to know the meaning of true and lasting happiness and how I could go about finding it."[1] Madonna has attempted to discover meaning in the ancient religion of Kabbalah.

Others have given up on finding meaning. Kurt Cobain, lead singer of the Seattle grunge band Nirvana, despaired of life at age twenty-seven and committed suicide.

Jazz-age cartoonist Ralph Barton also found life to be meaningless, leaving the following suicide note: "I have had few difficulties, many friends, great successes; I have gone from wife to wife, and from house to house, visited countries of the world, but I am fed up with inventing devices to fill up 24 hours of the day."[2]

All of us are looking to understand our condition and our destiny. So, what did Jesus say about our identity and the reason for our existence? Let's look at four truths Jesus told about who we are.

WE WERE MADE FOR A RELATIONSHIP WITH GOD

If you were to read through the New Testament Gospels, you would discover that Jesus continually spoke of our immense value to God, telling us that God created us to dwell with him eternally in a special home he is preparing for each of his children.[3]

After reading the Bible and considering what it says about our value to God, Bono was awestruck. He remarked in an interview, "It's a mind-blowing concept that the God who created the universe might be looking for company, a real relationship with people."[4] In other words, before the universe was created, God planned to adopt us into his family. Not only that, but he has also planned an incredible inheritance that is ours for the taking. Like the father's heart in Jesus' story, God wants to lavish on us an inheritance of unimaginable blessing and royal privilege.[5] In his eyes, we are special.

WE HAVE THE FREEDOM TO CHOOSE

In the movie *The Stepford Wives*, weak, lying, greedy, and murderous men have engineered submissive, obedient robots to replace their liberated wives, whom they considered threats. Although the men supposedly loved their wives, they replaced them with toys in order to force their obedience.

God could have made us like that—robotic people hardwired to love and obey him, programming worship into us like a screensaver. But then our compulsory love would be meaningless.

God wanted us to love him freely. In real relationships, we want someone to love us for who we are, not out of compulsion—we'd prefer a soul mate over a mail-order bride.

Søren Kierkegaard summarized the dilemma in this story.

> Suppose there was a king who loved a humble maiden. The king was like no other king. Every statesman trembled before his power . . . and yet this mighty king was melted by love for a humble maiden. How could he declare his love for her? In an odd sort of way, his kingliness tied his hands. If he brought her to the palace and crowned her head with jewels . . . she would surely not resist—no one dared resist him. But would she love him? She would say she loved him of course, but would she truly?[6]

You see the problem. Less poetically put: How do you break up with an all-knowing boyfriend? ("It's just not working out between us, but I guess you already knew that.") But to make freely exchanged love possible, God created human beings with a unique capacity: free will.

Jesus confirmed the fact that we have this freedom to choose by his many admonitions, such as "Repent," "Believe," "Follow me," "Come unto me," "Keep my commands," "Love one another," and "Abide in me."[7] These commands of Jesus demonstrate the fact that we have been created with freedom to choose God's ways or to rebel against him.

WE ARE REBELS AGAINST GOD'S MORAL LAWS

C. S. Lewis reasoned that even though we are internally programmed with a desire to know God, we rebel against it from the moment we are born.[8] Lewis also began to examine his own motives, which led him to the discovery that he instinctively knew right from wrong.

As a deep thinker, Lewis then wondered where this sense of right and wrong came from. We all experience this sense of right and wrong when we read of Hitler killing six million Jews or of a hero sacrificing his or her life for someone. We instinctively know it is wrong to lie and cheat. This recognition that we are programmed with an inner moral law led the former atheist to the conclusion that there must be a Lawgiver.

Indeed, according to both Jesus' teachings and the rest of the Scriptures, God has given us a moral law to obey. And not only have we turned our backs on a relationship with him, but we also have broken the moral laws that God established. Most of us know some of the Ten Commandments: "Don't lie, steal, murder, commit adultery," and so on. Jesus summarized them by saying we should love God with all our heart and our neighbor as ourselves.[9] Sin, therefore, is not only the wrong that we do in breaking the law, but also our failure to do what is right.

God made the universe with laws that govern everything in it. They are inviolable and unchangeable. When Einstein derived the formula $E=MC^2$, he took a step toward unlocking the mystery of nuclear energy. Put the right ingredients together under exacting conditions, and enormous power is unleashed. The Scriptures tell us that God's moral law is no less valid, since it stems from his very character.

From the very first man and woman, we have disobeyed God's laws, even though they are for our best. And we have failed to do what is right. We have inherited this condition from the first man, Adam. The Bible calls this disobedience *sin*, which means "missing the mark," like an archer missing his intended target. Thus our sins have broken God's intended relationship with us. Using the archer's example, we have missed the mark when it comes to the purpose for which we were created.

Sin causes the severing of all relationships: the human race severed from its environment (alienation), individuals severed from themselves (guilt and shame), people severed from other people (war, murder), and people severed from God (spiritual death). Like links on a chain, once the first link between God and humanity was broken, all contingent links became uncoupled.

And we are broken. As Kanye West raps, "And I don't think there's nothing I can do to right my wrongs . . . . I wanna talk to God, but I'm afraid 'cause we ain't spoke in so long." West's lyrics speak of the separation that sin brings to our lives. And according to the Bible, this separation is more than just lyrics in a rap song. It has deadly consequences.

WE ARE SEPARATED FROM GOD'S LOVE

Our rebellion (sin) has created a wall of separation between God and us.[10] In the Scriptures, "separation" means spiritual death. And spiritual death means being completely separated from the light and life of God. Jesus illustrated this separation from God in his story of Lazarus and the rich man, which speaks of a "great gulf" that separated the righteous Lazarus from the wicked rich man after each had died.[11]

Since we are unable to experience the real life God created us to have, we struggle to find meaning in other ways, such as through money, success, pleasure, or popularity. But none of these will fill the void caused by our separation from God.

"But wait a minute," you might say. "Didn't God know all of that before he made us? Why didn't he see that his plan was doomed for failure?"

Of course an all-knowing God would realize that we would rebel and sin. In fact, it is our failure that makes his plan so mind-blowing.

Rather than giving up on us, God's plan all along was to demonstrate his love for us in spite of the fact we didn't deserve it.

But is there anything God can do to fill this inner void brought about by our separation from him? This brings us to the reason that God came to earth in human form. And even more incredible—the remarkable reason for Jesus' death.

Chapter 9

WHAT DID JESUS SAY
ABOUT HIMSELF?

P ASCAL, THE GREAT French philosopher, believed this inner void we all experience can only be filled by God. He stated, "There is a God-shaped vacuum in the heart of every man which only Jesus Christ can fill."[1] If Pascal is right, then we would expect Jesus not only to answer the question of our identity and meaning in this life but also to give us hope for life after we die.

Can there be meaning without God? Not according to atheist Bertrand Russell, who wrote, "Unless you assume a god, the question of life's purpose is meaningless."[2] Russell resigned himself to ultimately rot in the grave. In his book, *Why I Am Not a Christian*, Russell dismissed everything Jesus said about life's meaning, including his promise of eternal life. He died a hopeless cynic.

So, who is the real Jesus? And is he able to fill the void in our lives now while giving us hope for eternal life after we die? To answer those questions, we need to understand Jesus' identity and qualifications in light of Old Testament prophecies.

HE IS GOD'S PERFECT SOLUTION

During his three years of public ministry, Jesus taught us how to live, and he performed many miracles, even raising the dead. But he stated that his mission was to save us from our sins.[3]

Jesus proclaimed that he was the promised Messiah who would take our iniquity upon himself. The prophet Isaiah had written about the Messiah seven hundred years earlier, giving us several clues regarding his identity. But the clue most difficult to grasp is that the Messiah would be *both man and God!* As one prophet predicted, "For to us a child is born, to us a son is given . . . . And he will be called . . . Mighty God, Everlasting Father, Prince of Peace."[4]

Author Ray Stedman writes of God's promised Messiah, "From the very beginning of the Old Testament, there is a sense of hope and expectation, like the sound of approaching footsteps: Someone is coming! . . . That hope increases throughout the prophetic record as prophet after prophet declares yet another tantalizing hint: Someone is coming!"[5]

WHAT DID JESUS SAY ABOUT HIMSELF?

The ancient prophet Isaiah had foretold that the Messiah would become God's perfect sin offering, satisfying his requirement of justice.[6] Hundreds of such prophecies spelled out sixty-one specific details that would be fulfilled by the Messiah when he arrived. Remarkably, Jesus fulfilled every one of them except those referring to his future return (visit Y-Jesus.com/Evidence3). According to God's Word spoken through the prophets, this promised Messiah would be the perfect man who would qualify to die for us.

The New Testament authors tell us that the only reason Jesus was qualified to die for the rest of us is because, as God, he lived a morally perfect life and wasn't subject to sin's judgment.[7]

It's difficult to understand how Jesus' death paid for our sins. Perhaps a judicial analogy might clarify how Jesus solves the dilemma of God's perfect love and justice.

Imagine entering a courtroom guilty of murder (you have some serious issues). As you approach the bench, you realize that the judge is your father. Knowing that he loves you, you immediately begin to plead, "Dad, just let me go!"

To which he responds, "I love you, son, but I'm a judge. I can't simply let you go."

He is torn. Eventually he bangs the gavel down and declares you guilty. Justice cannot be compromised, at least not by a judge. But because he loves you, he steps down from the bench, takes off his robe, and offers to pay the penalty for you. And, in fact, he takes your place in the electric chair.

This is the picture painted by the New Testament. God stepped down into human history, in the person of Jesus Christ, and went to the electric chair (read: cross) instead of us, and on our behalf. Jesus is not a third-party whipping boy, taking our sins, but rather he is God himself. Put more bluntly, God had two choices: to judge sin in us or to assume the punishment himself. In Christ, he chose the latter.

As an entertainer, Bono doesn't pretend to be a theologian. But in his understanding of the New Testament, he accurately states the reason for Jesus' death: "The point of the death of Christ is that Christ took on the sins of the world, so that what we put out did not come back to us, and that our sinful nature does not reap the obvious death. That's the point. It should keep us humbled. It's not our own good works that get us through the gates of Heaven."[8]

Bono is merely stating what the writers of the New Testament have told us. It was God's plan all along to send Jesus to save us. It was his way of demonstrating how much he loves us. And Jesus made it clear that he is the only one who can bring us to God, stating, "I am the way and the truth and the life. No one comes to the Father except through me."[9]

WHAT DID JESUS SAY ABOUT HIMSELF?

Many argue that Jesus' claim that he is the only way to God is too narrow, saying that there are many ways to God. Those who believe all religions are the same deny we have a sin problem. They refuse to take Christ's words seriously. They say God's love will accept all of us, regardless what we have done.

Perhaps Hitler or Osama bin Laden are deserving of judgment, they reason, but not themselves or others who live "decent lives." It's like saying that God grades on the curve, and everybody who gets a D- or better will get in. But this presents a dilemma.

As we have seen, sin is the absolute opposite of God's holy character. Thus we have offended the one who created us and loved us enough to sacrifice his very Son for us. In a sense, our rebellion is like spitting in his face. Neither good deeds, religion, meditation, nor karma can pay the debt our sins have incurred. Furthermore, it would be a violation of God's holy character to permit sin to go unpunished. Either we must suffer the penalty demanded by God's perfect justice, or someone else who is qualified must take the punishment for us.

According to theologian R. C. Sproul, Jesus alone is the one who can pay that debt. He writes, "Moses could meditate on the law; Muhammad could brandish a sword; Buddha could give personal counsel; Confucius could offer wise sayings; but none of these men was qualified to offer an atonement for the sins of the world . . . . Christ alone is worthy of unlimited devotion and service."[10]

He Is a Gift Undeserved

The biblical term to describe God's free forgiveness through Christ's sacrificial death is *grace*. Whereas mercy saves us from what we deserve, the grace of God gives us what we don't deserve. As a result of Jesus' sacrificial death, God's mercy saves us from the punishment we deserve. But far beyond that, his grace lavishes upon us an inheritance we don't deserve. Let's review for a minute how Christ has done for us what we could not do for ourselves:

- God loves us and created us for a relationship with himself.[11]
- We have been given the freedom to accept or reject that relationship.[12]
- Our sin and rebellion against God and his laws have created a wall of separation between us and him.[13]
- Though we are deserving of eternal judgment, God has paid our debt in full by Jesus' death in our place, making eternal life with him possible.[14]

What Did Jesus Say About Himself?

Recognizing his own need for grace, Bono gives us his perspective:

> Grace defies reason and logic. Love interrupts, if you like, the consequences of your actions, which in my case is very good news indeed, because I've done a lot of stupid stuff . . . . I'd be in big trouble if Karma was going to finally be my judge . . . . It doesn't excuse my mistakes, but I'm holding out for Grace. I'm holding out that Jesus took my sins onto the Cross, because I know who I am, and I hope I don't have to depend on my own religiosity.[15]

Bono's understanding of what Jesus was saying is that he could do for us what neither we nor anyone else could do.

We now have the picture of God's plan of the ages coming together. But there still is one missing ingredient. According to Jesus and the authors of the New Testament, each of us individually must respond to the free gift Jesus offers us. He won't force us to take it.

Part 4

CONCLUSION

Chapter 10

YOU CHOOSE
THE ENDING

WE CONTINUALLY MAKE choices—what to wear, what to eat, what kind of career to have, whom to marry, and so on. It is the same when it comes to a relationship with God. Author Ravi Zacharias writes, "Jesus' message reveals that every individual . . . comes to know God not by virtue of birth, but by a conscious choice to let Him have His rule in his or her individual life."[1]

Our choices are often influenced by others. However, in some instances we are given the wrong advice. On September 11, 2001, six hundred innocent people put their trust in the wrong advice and unfortunately suffered the consequences. The true story goes like this:

> One man who was on the 92nd floor of the south tower of the World Trade Center had just heard a jet crashing into the north tower.

Stunned by the explosion, he called the police for instructions on what to do. "We need to know if we need to get out of here, because we know there's an explosion," he said urgently on the phone.

The voice on the other end advised him not to evacuate. "I would wait 'til further notice."

"All right," the caller said. "Don't evacuate." He then hung up.

Shortly after 9:00 A.M., another jet crashed into the 80th floor of the south tower. Nearly all 600 people in the top floors of the south tower perished. The failure to evacuate the building was one of the day's great tragedies.[2]

Those six hundred people perished because they relied on the wrong information, even though it was given by a person who was trying to help. The tragedy would not have occurred if the six hundred victims had been given the right information.

Jesus claims to be the only way to God. We can either put our trust in him or mistakenly rely on the words of others. Our conscious choice about Jesus is infinitely more important than the one facing the ill-informed 9/11 victims. Eternity is at stake. We can choose one of three different responses:

1. We can ignore him.
2. We can reject him.
3. Or we can accept him.

Ignoring Jesus

The reason many people go through life ignoring God is that they are too busy pushing their own agenda. Chuck Colson was like that. At age thirty-nine, Colson occupied the office next to the president of the United States. He was the "tough guy" of the Nixon White House, the "hatchet man" who could make the hard decisions. Yet, in 1972, the Watergate scandal ruined his reputation, and his world became unglued. Later he wrote:

> I had been concerned with myself. I had done this and that, I had achieved, I had succeeded and I had given God none of the credit, never once thanking Him for any of His gifts to me. I had never thought of anything being "immeasurably superior" to myself, or if I had in fleeting moments thought about the infinite power of God, I had not related Him to my life.[3]

Many can identify with Colson. It's easy to get caught in the fast pace of life and have little or no time for God. Yet ignoring God's gracious offer of forgiveness has the same dire consequences as outright rejection. Our sin debt would still remain unpaid.

REJECTING JESUS

In criminal cases, few ever turn down a full pardon. But it's happened.

In 1915, George Burdick, city editor for the *New York Tribune*, had refused to reveal sources and had broken the law. President Woodrow Wilson declared a full pardon to Burdick for all offenses he had "committed or may have committed." What made Burdick's case historic is that he refused the pardon. That brought the case to the Supreme Court, which sided with Burdick, stating that a presidential pardon could not be forced on anyone.

When it comes to rejecting Christ's full pardon, people give a variety of reasons. Many say there isn't sufficient evidence, but like Bertrand Russell and a host of other cynical skeptics, they aren't interested enough to really investigate. Others refuse to look beyond some hypocritical Christians they know, pointing to unloving or inconsistent behavior as an excuse. And still others reject Christ because they blame God for some sad or tragic experience they have suffered.

However, Ravi Zacharias, who has debated with intellectuals on hundreds of college campuses, believes that the real reason most people reject God is moral. He writes, "A man rejects God neither because of intellectual demands nor because of the scarcity of evidence. A man rejects God because of moral resistance that refuses to admit his need for God."[4]

Accepting Jesus

The desire for moral freedom kept C. S. Lewis from God for most of his college years. Lewis explained how acceptance of Christ involves more than just intellectual agreement with the facts. "Fallen man is not simply an imperfect creature who needs improvement: he is a rebel who must lay down his arms. Laying down your arms, surrendering, saying you are sorry, realizing that you have been on the wrong track and getting ready to start life over again . . . is what Christians call repentance."[5]

"Repentance" is a word that means a dramatic turnaround in thinking. That's what happened to Nixon's former "hatchet man." After Watergate was exposed, Colson began thinking about life differently. Sensing his own lack of purpose, he began reading Lewis's *Mere Christianity*, given to him by a friend. Trained as a lawyer, Colson took out a yellow legal pad and began writing down Lewis's arguments. Colson recalled, "I knew the time had come for me. Was I to accept without reservations Jesus Christ as Lord of my life? It was like a gate before me. There was no way to walk around it. I would step through, or I would remain outside. A 'maybe' or 'I need more time' was kidding myself."

After an inner struggle, this former aide to the president of the United States finally realized that Jesus Christ was deserving of his full allegiance. "And so early Friday morning, while I sat alone staring at the sea I love, words I had not been certain I could understand or say fell naturally from my lips: 'Lord Jesus, I believe You. I accept You. Please come into my life. I commit it to You.'"[6]

Colson discovered that his questions "Who am I?", "Why am I here?", and "Where am I going?" are all answered in a personal relationship with Jesus Christ. He discovered the "secret" that the apostle Paul wrote of nearly 2,000 years ago: "May . . . you see more and more fully God's great secret, Christ himself! For it is in *him,* and in him alone, that men will find all the treasures of wisdom and knowledge."[7]

Jesus Christ is the answer to all our needs. When we enter into a personal relationship with him, he fills our inner void, gives us peace, and satisfies our desire for meaning and hope. And we no longer need to resort to temporary experiences for our fulfillment. When he enters into us, he also satisfies our deepest longings and needs for true, lasting love and security.

And the staggering thing is that God himself came as a man to pay our entire debt. Therefore, no longer are we under the penalty of sin. Paul states this clearly to the Colossians when he writes, "You were his enemies, separated from him by your evil thoughts and actions. Yet now he has reconciled you to himself through the death of Christ in his physical body. As a result, he has brought you into his own presence, and you are holy and blameless as you stand before him without a single fault."[8]

Thus God did for us what we were unable to do for ourselves. We are set free from our sins by Jesus' sacrificial death. It is like a mass murderer going before a judge and being granted a full and complete pardon. Guilty of murder, he doesn't deserve a pardon, and as sinners, neither do we. God's gift of eternal life is absolutely free—and it is for the taking. But even though the pardon is offered to us, it is up to us to accept it.

The Choice Is Yours

Are you at a point in your life where you would like to accept God's free offer?

Perhaps like Bono, Lewis, and Colson, your life has also been empty. Nothing you have tried satisfies the inner void you feel. God can fill that void and change you in a moment. He created you to have life that is flooded with meaning and purpose. Jesus said, "My purpose is to give . . . a rich and satisfying life."[9]

Or perhaps things are going well for you in life, but you are restless and lack peace. You realize that you have broken God's laws and are separated from his love and forgiveness. You fear God's judgment. Jesus said, "I am leaving you with a gift—peace of mind and heart. And the peace I give is a gift the world can't give."[10] So whether you are simply tired of a life of empty pursuits or are troubled by a lack of peace with your creator, the answer is in Jesus Christ.

When you put your trust in Jesus Christ, God will forgive you of all your sins and make you his child. As his child, you will have purpose and meaning in life on earth and the promise of eternal life with him.

God's Word says, "To all who believed [Jesus Christ] and accepted him, he gave the right to become children of God."[11]

Forgiveness of sin, purpose in life, and eternal life are all yours for the asking. You can invite Christ into your life right now by faith through prayer. Prayer is talking with God. God knows your heart and is not as concerned with your words as he is with the attitude of your heart. The following is a suggested prayer:

> Dear God, I want to know you personally and live eternally with you. Thank you, Lord Jesus, for dying on the cross for my sins. I open the door of my life and receive you as my Savior and Lord. Take control of my life and change me, making me the kind of person you want me to be.

Does this prayer express the desire of your heart? If so, simply pray the above suggested prayer in your own words.

When you make a commitment to Jesus Christ, he enters your life, becoming your guide, your counselor, your comforter, and your best friend.

Furthermore, he gives you strength to overcome trials and temptation, freeing you to experience a new life full of meaning, purpose, and power.

What an amazing plan that God has designed! It is a plan that elevates the human spirit and provides inner peace, meaning, and hope, regardless of the circumstances we face in life. And as the apostle Paul tells the Ephesians, it is a plan that includes us, with Jesus Christ as its central theme.

> Praise be to God . . . . For consider what he has done—before the foundation of the world he chose us to become, in Christ, holy and blameless children living within his constant care. He planned, in his purpose of love, that we should be adopted as his own children through Jesus Christ . . . .

> It is through the Son, at the cost of his own blood, that we are redeemed, freely forgiven through that full and generous grace which has overflowed into our lives and opened our eyes to the truth. For God has allowed us to know the secret of his plan, and it is this: he purposes in his sovereign will that all human history shall be consummated in Christ, that everything that exists in Heaven or earth shall find its perfection and fulfillment in him.

> And here is the staggering thing—that in all which will one day belong to him we have been promised a share. [12]

A New Beginning

This is indeed staggering news: No matter what you have done, God is offering you a full pardon and a new beginning with his Son. He carries no grudges over your past failures, and because of Christ's sacrifice, he sees you as totally righteous. God loves you and is ready to throw his royal robes around you and celebrate like the father in the parable did with his wayward son. Paul writes of this wonderful new beginning. "This means that anyone who belongs to Christ has become a new person. The old life is gone; a new life has begun!"[13]

Perhaps you are thinking that as a Christian you now need to live this new life with Christ in your own strength. But the Bible tells us just the opposite: It tells us that you can't do it—but he can. When you invite him in, Jesus enters your life, and as you commit yourself to him, he gives you the necessary power to live obediently. It is a matter of yielding and trusting him.

Once we grasp the high price Jesus paid to have us as God's children, our lives should never be the same. As his child, you will still experience temptation, and there may be times of doubt and failure. But he will never give up on you or disown you.[14] In fact, he gives you the power to live for him.

And no matter what you go through in life, God will always be there for you. Paul tells the

Philippians, "Being confident of this, that he who began a good work in you will carry it on to completion until the day of Christ Jesus."[15]

If you are ready to begin this new life with Christ, we encourage you to review God's wonderful promises and growth principles in Appendix A.

Appendix A

WHAT DOES JESUS
DO FOR YOU?

NEW LIFE IN CHRIST

IF YOU HAVE made the decision to receive Jesus Christ as your personal Savior and Lord, you are God's child for all eternity.[1] As his child, you are given an inheritance that includes the following wonderful promises:

1. Jesus enters your life in the person of the Holy Spirit, never to leave.[2]
2. Jesus' death pays for all your sins.[3]
3. Jesus gives you eternal life with him in heaven.[4]
4. Jesus assures that your prayers are heard and answered.[5]
5. Jesus gives you power to obey him by faith.[6]

RECEIVING JESUS' UNCONDITIONAL LOVE

Jesus promises to indwell you and be your friend and Lord forever.[7] His love is not based on how you perform or how you feel. The emotional high you might experience now won't always be there, but Jesus will be.

Youth leader Samantha Tidball tells how, when she was a teenager, she dated a number of guys and repeatedly found herself bored after a few weeks of dating. She realized that she got an emotional high from the chase—one that wasn't sustainable. And she says it was sort of the same thing when she first began a relationship with God. When the initial emotional rush was over, she felt empty inside and continued looking for attention elsewhere. She knew God loved her, but she didn't always feel his love.

She wrote in a blog:

> I have learned that I can't force a feeling. But I can reflect on what I know and trust that God truly does love me. I have to trust Jesus meant what He said in 1 John 4:9–10, "God showed how much He loved us by sending His one and only Son into the World so that we might have eternal life through Him. This is real love—not that we loved God, but that he loved us and sent His Son as a sacrifice to take away our sins." If Jesus died for you and me, then what does that say about our

self-worth? Jesus says, "There is no greater love than to lay down one's life for one's friends" (John 15:13). Apparently, God loves us enough to die for us; there is no greater act of love.

God loves us just the way we are. Living better lives or thinking deeper thoughts will never make him love us more than he already does. Tidball says, "Don't confuse God's love with the love you get from people. Love from people often increases with performance and decreases with mistakes. Not so with God's love. He loves you right where you are."[8]

MAKING YOUR LIFE COUNT FOR HIM

As you consider what Jesus has done for you, you will want to turn your life over to him so he can make it count for him. The apostle Paul puts it this way: "Christ's love compels us, because we are convinced that one died for all, and therefore all died. And he died for all, that those who live should no longer live for themselves but for him who died for them and was raised again."[9]

Once you begin your new journey with Christ, his Holy Spirit begins to change you—as you yield to him—into the person he planned you to be. But don't expect immediate perfection; the Christian life is more like a marathon than a sprint. The best runners always spend hours in training. Training in the Christian life involves seven basic areas:

1. Acknowledge Jesus is always in your life.
2. Trust him with each area of your life.
3. Spend time reading and studying the Bible.
4. Talk with him in prayer.
5. Yield to him in obedience to his Word.
6. Fellowship with other believers.
7. Share his love and grace with others.

We encourage you to download the free resource "Getting Started in Extreme Living," which will help you understand how to exercise and apply these vital areas of Christian growth. Go to Y-Jesus.com/download. Other free downloadable resources and online Bibles are available at GodResources.org/NewLife.

Appendix B

ARE THE GOSPELS TRUE?

ARE THE NEW Testament Gospels the true eyewitness history of Jesus Christ, or could the story have been changed through the years? Must we simply take the New Testament accounts of Jesus by faith, or is there actual evidence for their reliability? To find out, we need to examine some facts from the past two thousand years.

We begin with two simple questions: When were the original documents of the New Testament written? And who wrote them?

The New Testament writers claimed to be rendering eyewitness accounts of Jesus. The apostle Peter stated it this way: "We were not making up clever stories when we told you about the power of our Lord Jesus Christ and his coming again. We have seen his majestic splendor with our own eyes."[1]

The apostle Paul's letters, dated between the mid-40s and the mid-60s (or around twelve to thirty-three years after Christ's death), constitute the earliest witnesses to Jesus' life and teaching.

One of the world's leading historians, Will Durant, wrote of the historical importance of Paul's letters: "The Christian evidence for Christ begins with the letters ascribed to Saint Paul . . . . No one has questioned the existence of Paul, or his repeated meetings with Peter, James, and John; and Paul enviously admits that these men had known Christ in the flesh."[2]

EARLY EVIDENCE

So, what evidence do we have concerning when the Gospel accounts of Jesus were really written? The consensus of most scholars is that the Gospels were written by apostles during the first century. Three primary forms of evidence appear to build a solid case for their conclusions:

- Early documents from heretics such as Marcion and the school of Valentinus citing New Testament books, themes, and passages[3]
- Numerous writings of early Christian sources, such as Clement of Rome, Ignatius, and Polycarp
- Discovered copies of Gospel fragments carbon-dated as early as AD 114[3]

Biblical archaeologist William Albright concluded on the basis of his research that all the New Testament books were written while most of the apostles were still alive. He wrote, "We can already say emphatically that there is no longer any solid basis for dating any book after about 80 AD, two full generations before the date of between 130 and 150 AD given by the more radical New Testament critics of today."[4] Elsewhere Albright put the writing of the entire New Testament at "very probably sometime between about 50 AD and 75 AD."[5]

The notoriously skeptical scholar John A. T. Robinson dates the New Testament between AD 40 and 65. That puts its writing as early as seven to ten years after Christ lived.[6] If that is true, any historical errors would have been immediately exposed by both eyewitnesses and the enemies of Christianity.

So let's look at the trail of clues that takes us from the original documents to our New Testament copies today.

WHO NEEDS A COPY MACHINE?

The original writings of the apostles were revered. Churches studied them, shared them, carefully preserved them, and stored them away like buried treasure.

As the number of churches multiplied, hundreds of copies were carefully made under the supervision of church leaders. Every letter was meticulously penned in ink on parchment or papyrus. And so, today, scholars can study the surviving copies (and the copies of copies, and the copies of copies of copies—you get it), to determine authenticity and arrive at a very close approximation of the original documents.

In fact, scholars studying ancient literature have devised the science of textual criticism to examine documents such as *The Odyssey*, comparing them with other ancient documents to determine their accuracy. It is a three-part test that looks at not only the faithfulness of the copy but also the credibility of the authors. The tests are these:

1. The bibliographical test
2. The internal evidence test
3. The external evidence test[7]

Let's see what happens when we apply these tests to the early New Testament manuscripts.

BIBLIOGRAPHICAL TEST

This test compares a document with other ancient history from the same period. It asks the following:

- How many copies of the original document are in existence?

- How large of a time gap is there between the original writings and the earliest copies?
- How well does a document compare with other ancient history?

So, how well does the New Testament compare with other ancient writings with regard to both the number of copies and the time gap from the originals?

Table A, on the next page, reveals the New Testament has far more copies in its original language (Greek) than any ancient secular historical writing, and the time gap between the original writings and known copies is significantly less.

When counting translations into other languages, the number is a staggering number of over twenty-four thousand partial or complete manuscripts—dating from the second to the fifteenth centuries.

Compare that with the second-best-documented ancient historical manuscript, Homer's *Iliad*, with 643 copies. And remember that most ancient historical works have far fewer existing manuscripts than that one does (usually fewer than ten). New Testament scholar Bruce Metzger remarked, "In contrast with these figures [of other ancient manuscripts], the textual critic of the New Testament is embarrassed by the wealth of his material."[9]

TABLE A[8]

AUTHOR BOOK	DATE WRITTEN	EARLIEST COPIES	TIME GAP	NO. COPIES
Homer Iliad	800 BC	c. 400 BC	c. 400 years	643
Herodotus History	480–425 BC	c. AD 900	c. 1,350 years	8
Thucydides History	460–400 BC	c. AD 900	c. 1,300 years	8
Plato Tetralogies	400 BC	c. AD 900	c. 1,300 years	7
Desmothenes	300 BC	c. AD 1100	c. 1,400 years	200
Caesar Gallic Wars	100–44 BC	c. AD 900	c. 1,000 years	10
Livy History of Rome	59 BC–AD 17	4th century (partial) mostly 10th century	c. 400 years c. 1,000 years	1 partial 19 copies mostly 10th century
Tacitus Annals	AD 100	c. AD 1100	c. 1,000 years	20
NEW TESTAMENT	AD 50–100	c. AD 114 (fragment) c. AD 200 (books) c. AD 250 (most of N.T.) c. AD 325 (complete N.T.)	+50 years 100 years 150 years 225 years	5,366

TIME GAP

Not only is the number of manuscripts significant, but so is the time gap between when the original was written and the date of the copy. Over the course of a thousand years of copying, there's no telling what a text could evolve into. But over a hundred years, that's a different story.

Of all *secular* ancient historical documents outlined in Table A, the shortest time span between the actual writings and the surviving copies is 750 years. The earliest copies of Caesar and Plato were written nine hundred years after their histories were written. Yet, their words are accepted as authentic, and most scholars would laugh at the suggestion that they were invalid.

Furthermore, the *Annals* by Tacitus is regarded as valid Roman history even though there is an enormous gap of a thousand years between the original documents and copies. In comparison, the earliest known copy of the New Testament dates to within a generation of when the original was penned.

When a cache of New Testament papyri fragments were discovered in Egypt, among them was a fragment of the Gospel of John [p_{52}] dated to A.D. 114–125. And the words on that fragment match what we have in our New Testaments today. This early manuscript, along with others dated slightly later, reveals that the words of the New Testament are much more reliable than what skeptics have argued.

Find after find, archeology has unearthed copies of major portions of the New Testament dated to within 150 years of the originals.

Most other ancient documents have time gaps of from four hundred to fourteen hundred years. For example, Aristotle's *Poetics* was written about 343 BC, yet the earliest copy is dated AD 1100, with only five copies in existence. And yet no one is going in search of the historical Plato, claiming he was actually a fireman and not a philosopher.

Even critical scholar John A. T. Robinson has admitted, "The wealth of manuscripts, and above all the narrow interval of time between the writing and the earliest extant copies, make it by far the best attested text of any ancient writing in the world."[10] Professor of law John Warwick Montgomery affirmed, "To be skeptical of the resultant text of the New Testament books is to allow all of classical antiquity to slip into obscurity, for no documents of the ancient period are as well attested bibliographically as the New Testament."[11]

The point is this: If the New Testament records were made and circulated so closely to the actual events, their portrayal of Jesus is most likely accurate. But such evidence is not the only way to answer the question of reliability. Scholars also use internal evidence to answer this question.

INTERNAL EVIDENCE TEST

Like good detectives, historians verify reliability by looking at internal clues. Such clues reveal motives of the authors and their willingness to disclose details and other features that could be verified. The key internal clues these scholars use to test for reliability include the following:

- consistency of eyewitness reports
- details of names, places, and events
- letters to individuals or small groups
- features embarrassing to the authors[12]

CONSISTENCY

Eyewitnesses to a crime or an accident generally get the big events right but see it from different perspectives. Likewise, the four Gospels describe the events of Jesus' life from different perspectives. Yet, regardless of these perspectives, Bible scholars are amazed at the consistency of their accounts and the clear picture of Jesus and his teaching they put together with their complementary reports.

Details

If the New Testament writings had been mere inventions of the apostles, phony names, places, and events would have quickly been spotted by their enemies, the Jewish and Roman leaders. Yet many of the New Testament details have been proved true by independent verification. Classical historian Colin Hemer, for example, "identifies 84 facts in the last 16 chapters of Acts that have been confirmed by archaeological research."[13]

Letters to Small Groups

Historical expert Louis Gottschalk notes that personal letters intended for small audiences have a high probability of being reliable.[14] Which category do the New Testament documents fall into? Well, some of them were clearly intended to be circulated widely. Yet large portions of the New Testament consist of personal letters written to small groups and individuals. These documents, at least, would not be considered prime candidates for falsification.

Embarrassing Features

Surprisingly, the authors of the New Testament presented themselves as all too frequently dim-witted, cowardly, and faithless. As respect for the apostles was crucial in the early church, inclusion of this kind of material doesn't make sense unless the apostles were reporting truthfully.[15]

EXTERNAL EVIDENCE TEST

The third and final measure of a document's reliability is the external evidence test, which asks, "Do historical records outside the New Testament confirm its reliability?" So, what did non-Christian historians say about Jesus Christ?

"Overall, at least nineteen non-Christian writings record more than fifty details concerning the life, teachings, death, and resurrection of Jesus, plus details concerning the early church."[16] This is astounding, considering the lack of other history we possess from this time period. Jesus is mentioned by more sources than the conquests of Caesar during this same period. It is even more astounding since these confirmations of New Testament details date from twenty to 150 years after Christ, "quite early by the standards of ancient historiography."[17]

The reliability of the New Testament is further substantiated by more than thirty-six thousand extra-biblical Christian documents (quotes from church leaders of the first three centuries) dating as early as ten years after the last writing of the New Testament.[18] If all the copies of the New Testament were lost, you could reproduce it from these other letters and documents with the exception of a few verses.[19]

Clark Pinnock, professor at McMaster Divinity College, summed it up well when he said, "There exists no document from the ancient world witnessed by so excellent a set of textual and historical testimonies . . . . An honest [person] cannot dismiss a source of this kind.

Skepticism regarding the historical credentials of Christianity is based upon an irrational basis."[20]

So, if the evidence supports the reliability of the New Testament, there can be little dispute about who its writers thought the real Jesus was. Whether or not they are right in their conclusions has been the subject of this book—and is the question each of us must answer for ourselves.

Endnotes

Introduction

1. The "Christ-myth" idea that originated in the late eighteenth century has been popularized more recently by conspiracy books as well as the movie, *Zeitgeist*. But the idea Jesus never existed is primarily promoted by conspiracy enthusiasts and antagonists to Christianity, not leading historians. It has been soundly rejected by leading scholars. New Testament scholar F. F. Bruce writes, "Some writers may toy with the fancy of a 'Christ-myth', but they do not do so on the ground of historical evidence. The historicity of Christ is as axiomatic for an unbiased historian as the historicity of Julius Caesar. It is not historians who propagate the 'Christ-myth' theories." F. F. Bruce, *The New Testament Documents: Are*

they Reliable? (Grand Rapids, MI: InterVarsity, 1997), 119. Atheist historian Michael Grant noted, "To sum up, modern critical methods fail to support the Christ-myth theory. It has 'again and again been answered and annihilated by first-rank scholars . . . . No serious scholar has ventured to postulate the non-historicity of Jesus—or at any rate very few, and they have not succeeded in disposing of the much stronger, indeed very abundant, evidence to the contrary.'"[1] Michael Grant, *Jesus* (London: Rigel, 2004), 200.

2. Quoted in "What Life Means to Einstein: An Interview by George Sylvester Viereck," *The Saturday Evening Post,* Oct. 26, 1929, 17.

3. For further evidence on the historical existence of Jesus Christ see, "Was Jesus a Real Person?" at Y-Jesus.com / Evidence4.

4. H. G. Wells, *The Outline of History* (New York: Doubleday, 1949), 528.

5. Gary R. Habermas and Michael R. Licona, *The Case for the Resurrection of Jesus* (Grand Rapids, MI: Kregel, 2004), 52–53, 233. ["There are, very clearly, at least nineteen early pagan writers who refer to Jesus Christ as an actual, real-life, historical figure: Tacitus, a great historian of Rome; Suetonius, also a historian; Pliny the Younger, one of the leaders of the Roman Empire; Epictetus; Lucian; Aristides; Galenus; Lampridius; Dio Cassius; Emeritus; Annianus

(or Anianus); Marcellinus; Eunapius; and Zosimus. Some wrote entire works about Jesus, such as Lucian, Celsus (the first great antagonist, who wrote a whole book attacking Christianity), Porphyry, Hieracles, and Julian the Apostate. D. James Kennedy, *Skeptics Answered* (Sisters, OR: Multnomah, 1997), 73.]

6. C. S. Lewis, *God in the Dock* (Grand Rapids, MI: Eerdmans, 2000), 160.

7. "Mona Lisa's Smirk," *Y-Jesus* magazine, see Y-Jesus.com/Evidence5.

8. F. F. Bruce, *The Books and the Parchments* (Old Tappan, NJ: Revell, 1984), 168.

9. Bruce M. Metzger, *The Text of the New Testament,* 3rd ed. (Oxford: Oxford University Press, 1992), 38–39.

10. Richard Dawkins, *A Devil's Chaplain: Reflections on Hope, Lies, Science, and Love* (Boston: Houghton Mifflin, 2003), 245.

11. Habermas and Licona, 90. The argument that Jesus' resurrection was copied from pagan religions would require these religions to predate Christianity. Yet, T. N. D. Mettinger, professor at Lund University, writes in his book, *The Riddle of Resurrection,* "The consensus among modern scholars—*nearly universal*—is that there were no dying and rising gods that preceded Christianity. They all post-dated the first century." Quoted in Lee Strobel, *The Case for the Real Jesus* (Grand Rapids, MI: Zondervan, 2007), 160.

12. Ibid., 91.
13. Ravi Zacharias, *Jesus Among Other Gods* (Nashville: Word, 2000), 55.

Chapter 1

1. Vinoth Ramachandra, *Gods That Fail* (London: Paternoster, 1996), 198.
2. God is revealed in the Bible as a tri-unity (Trinity). Although he is one in essence, he exists in three distinct persons: Father, Son and Holy Spirit. Trinitarian teaching does *not* mean there are three Gods. The God of the Bible is revealed as infinitely more complex than the human mind is able to grasp. According to the teaching of the apostles, Jesus is fully God, but not *all* of God. The New Testament teaches that Jesus existed eternally with his Father and the Holy Spirit, and is the very creator of the universe (John 1:3; Colossians 1:15–17; Hebrews 1:2–12). However, he put aside his "divine prerogatives" to become a man (Philippians 2:5–11). The New Testament reveals Jesus as fully God and fully man. His humanity was additional to his divine nature, not in place of it. That is why some verses in the New Testament speak of his humanity, while others refer to his deity. To read more on what the New Testament says about Jesus' deity see: Y-Jesus.com/Evidence5 and Y-Jesus.com/Evidence 6.

3. Quoted in Terrence J. Rynne, *Gandhi and Christianity* (Maryknoll, NY: Orbis, 2008).

4. Joseph Klausner, *Jesus of Nazareth* (New York: Macmillan, 1946), 43–44.

5. Will Durant, *The Story of Philosophy* (New York: Washington Square, 1961), 428.

6. Linda Kulman and Jay Tolson, "The Jesus Code," *U. S. News & World Report*, December 22, 2003, 1.

7. Ravi Zacharias, *Jesus Among Other Gods* (Nashville: Word, 2000), 89.

8. Ramachandra, 199.

9. C. S. Lewis, *God in the Dock* (Grand Rapids, MI: Eerdmans, 2000), 160.

10. Quoted in Peter Kreeft and Ronald K. Tacelli, *Handbook of Christian Apologetics* (Downers Grove, IL: InterVarsity Press, 1994), 150.

Chapter 2

1. John Piper, *The Pleasures of God* (Sisters, OR: Multnomah, 2000), 35.

2. *Why I Am a Christian,* Norman L. Geisler, Paul K. Hoffman, editors, Peter Kreeft, "Why I Believe Jesus is the Son of God" (Grand Rapids, MI: Baker Books, 2001), 223.

3. Quoted in Timothy Keller, *The Reason for God* (New York: Penguin, 2008), 229.

4. John 17:3.

5. John 14:9.

6. John 8:58; 11:25; 8:12; 14:6.

7. *Ego eimi* is the Greek equivalent of the Hebrew name used to describe God in Isaiah 43:10–11. Dr. James White notes, "The closest and most logical connection between John's usage of *ego eimi* and the Old Testament is to be found in the Septuagint rendering of a particular Hebrew phrase, *ani hu* in the writings (primarily) of Isaiah. The Septuagint translates the Hebrew phrase *ani hu* as *ego eimi* in Isaiah 41:4, 43:10 and 46:4" (aomin.org/EGO.html). See also "Did Jesus Claim to Be God?" Y-Jesus.com/Evidence7.
8. John 10:33.
9. C. S. Lewis, *Mere Christianity* (San Francisco: Harper, 2001), 51.
10. Ibid.
11. A deist is someone who believes in an absentee God—a deity who created the world and then lets it run according to preestablished laws. Deism was a fad among intellectuals around the time of America's independence, and Jefferson bought into it.
12. Lewis, 52.

Chapter 3

1. J. I. Packer, *Knowing God* (Downers Grove, IL: InterVarsity Press, 1993), 57.
2. Philip Schaff, *The Person of Christ: The Miracle of History* (New York: American Tract Society, 1913), 94–95.

3. C. S. Lewis, *Mere Christianity* (San Francisco: Harper, 2001), 52.
4. Quoted in Schaff, 98–99.
5. Quoted in Timothy Keller, *The Reason for God* (New York: Penguin, 2008), 229.
6. C. S. Lewis, *God in the Dock* (Grand Rapids, MI: Eerdmans, 2000), 156.
7. Ibid.
8. Lewis, *Mere Christianity*, 52.

Chapter 4

1. John 11:25.
2. Quoted in Paul Edwards, "Great Minds: Bertrand Russell," *Free Inquiry*, December 2004–January 2005, 46.
3. R. C. Sproul, *Reason to Believe* (Grand Rapids, MI: Lamplighter, 1982), 44.
4. Josh McDowell, *The New Evidence That Demands a Verdict* (San Bernardino, CA: Here's Life, 1999), 203.
5. Bertrand Russell, *Why I Am Not a Christian* (New York: Simon & Schuster, 1957), 16; Joseph Campbell, an interview with Bill Moyers, *Joseph Campbell and the Power of Myth*, PBS, 1988; Michael J. Wilkins and J. P. Moreland, eds., *Jesus Under Fire* (Grand Rapids, MI: Zondervan, 1995), 2.
6. "What Is a Skeptic?" editorial in *Skeptic* 11, no. 2, 5.

7. Wilbur M. Smith, *A Great Certainty in This Hour of World Crises* (Wheaton, IL: Van Kampen, 1951), 10–11.

8. The Aramaic word Jesus uttered, *tetelestai*, is an accounting term meaning "debt paid in full," referring to the debt of our sins.

9. Matthew 27:45 tells of a period of darkness during Jesus' final three hours on the cross. Jesus' death was followed by an earthquake that tore the Temple Veil, a large curtain that had separated the sacred Holy of Holies from the people (v. 51). Jesus' death removed the wall of separation between God and man represented by the Temple Veil (Hebrews 9:1–9 and 10:19–22).

   Historian Will Durant reported, "About the middle of this first century a pagan named Thallus . . . argued that the abnormal darkness alleged to have accompanied the death of Christ was a purely natural phenomenon and coincidence; the argument took the existence of Christ for granted. The denial of that existence never seems to have occurred even to the bitterest gentile or Jewish opponents of nascent Christianity." Will Durant, *Caesar and Christ*, vol. 3 of The Story of Civilization (New York: Simon & Schuster, 1972), 555.

10. Vinoth Ramachandra, *Gods That Fail* (London: Paternoster, 1996), 198.

11. Jim Bishop, *The Day Christ Died* (New York: Harper Collins, 1977), 257.

12. Quoted in Lee Strobel, *The Case for Christ* (Grand Rapids, MI: Zondervan, 1998), 246.

Chapter 5

1. Peter Steinfels, "Jesus Died—And Then What Happened?" *New York Times*, April 3, 1988.
2. William D. Edwards et al, "On the Physical Death of Jesus Christ," *Journal of the American Medical Association*, 255, no. 11.
3. Lucian of Samosata, "The Passing of Peregrinus," tertullian.org/rpearse/lucian/peregrinus.htm.
4. Flavius Josephus, *Antiquities of the Jews* (Grand Rapids, MI: Kregel, 1966), 379. A portion of Josephus's comments about Jesus are disputed by critics, believing them to have been altered. However, his confirmation of both Jesus' existence and his reference to Pilate condemning him to the cross are deemed authentic by most scholars. Copies under Islamic control as well as Christian copies of his work cite Jesus' crucifixion under Pilate as an historical event. Since these copies were not under Christian control, the argument that they were altered by Christian scholars is flawed. Therefore, most scholars accept Josephus' account of Jesus in them as reliable.
5. Tacitus, *Annals,* 15, 44, as quoted in *The Annals and The Histories by Cornelius Tacitus*, ed. Robert Maynard Hutchins, vol. 15 of

Great Books of the Western World (Chicago: William Benton, 1952).

6. Quoted in Gary R. Habermas and Michael R. Licona, *The Case for the Resurrection of Jesus* (Grand Rapids, MI: Kregel, 2004), 49.

7. Frank Morison, *Who Moved the Stone?* (Grand Rapids, MI: Lamplighter, 1958), 9.

8. Paul L. Maier, *Independent Press Telegram* (Long Beach, CA), April 21, 1973.

9. Josh McDowell, *The Resurrection Factor Part 3*, Josh McDowell Ministries, 2009, http://www.bethinking.org/bible-jesus/intermediate/the-resurrection-factor-part-3.htm

10. Quoted in Josh McDowell, *The Resurrection Factor* (San Bernardino, CA: Here's Life, 1981), 66.

11. Paul Johnson, *A History of the Jews* (New York: Harper & Row, 1988), 130.

12. John W. Montgomery, *History and Christianity* (Downers Grove, IL: InterVarsity Press, 1971), 78.

13. Norman L. Geisler and Frank Turek, *I Don't Have Enough Faith to Be an Atheist* (Wheaton, IL: Crossway, 2004), 243.

14. Acts 10:39–41 (NLT).

15. Michael Green, *The Empty Cross of Jesus* (Downers Grove, IL: InterVarsity Press, 1984), 97.

16. Paul Little, *Know Why You Believe* (Wheaton, IL: Victor, 1967), 44.

17. J. P. Moreland, *Scaling the Secular City*, (Grand Rapids, MI: Baker, 2000), 172.

18. Charles Colson, "The Paradox of Power," Power to Change, powertochange.ie/changed/index_Leaders.

19. Morison, 104.

20. Quoted in Lee Strobel, *The Case for Christ* (Grand Rapids, MI: Zondervan, 1998), 238.

21. Thomas James Thorburn, *The Resurrection Narratives and Modern Criticism* (London: Kegan Paul, Trench, Trubner & Co., 1910), 158–9.

22. A. N. Sherwin-White, *Roman Society and Roman Law in the New Testament* (Oxford: Clarendon, 1963), 188–91.

23. Habermas and Licona, 85.

24. Ibid., 52–53.

25. Ibid., 87.

Chapter 6

1. Frank Morison, *Who Moved the Stone?* (Grand Rapids, MI: Lamplighter, 1958), 115.

2. J. N. D. Anderson, "The Resurrection of Jesus Christ," *Christianity Today*, April 1968, 12.

3. Morison, 9.

4. C. S. Lewis, *God in the Dock* (Grand Rapids, MI: Eerdmans, 2000), 159.

5. Simon Greenleaf, *The Testimony of the Evangelists Examined by the Rules of Evidence Administered in Courts of Justice* (1874; reprint, Grand Rapids, MI: Kregel, 1995), back cover.

6. Ibid., 32.
7. Ibid., back cover.

Chapter 7

1. Josh McDowell, *More than a Carpenter* (Wheaton, IL: Tyndale, 1977), 121.
2. Matthew 6:8.
3. Luke 15:11–32.
4. John 17:11.
5. J. I. Packer, *Knowing God*, (Downers Grove, IL: InterVarsity Press, 1993), 158.

Chapter 8

1. "Oprah talks to Madonna," *O: The Oprah Magazine*, January 2004, 120.
2. Quoted in Josh McDowell, *The Resurrection Factor* (San Bernardino, CA: Here's Life, 1981), 1.
3. John 3:16; 14:1–2.
4. Quoted in Michka Assayas, *Bono in Conversation* (New York: Riverhead, 2005), 203.
5. Luke 11:13; 1 John 3:1
6. Søren Kierkegaard, *Philosophical Fragments*, trans. Howard V. Hong and Edna H. Hong (Princeton, NJ: Princeton University Press, 1985), 26–28.
7. Luke 13:3; Mark 5:36; Matthew 4:19; 11:28; John 14:21; 13:34; 15:4.
8. C. S. Lewis, *Mere Christianity* (San Francisco: Harper, 2001), 160.

9. Matthew 22:37–39 (compare Exodus 20:1–17).
10. Isaiah 59:2.
11. Luke 16:19–31.

Chapter 9

1. Quoted in William R. Bright, *Jesus and the Intellectual* (San Bernardino, CA: Here's Life, 1968), 33.
2. Quoted in Rick Warren, *The Purpose Driven Life* (Grand Rapids, MI: Zondervan, 2002), 17.
3. Luke 19:10.
4. Isaiah 9:6.
5. Ray C. Stedman, *God's Loving Word* (Grand Rapids, MI: Discovery House, 1993), 50.
6. Isaiah 53:5–6.
7. Romans 5:8–21.
8. Quoted in Michka Assayas, *Bono in Conversation* (New York: Riverhead, 2005), 204.
9. John 14:6.
10. R. C. Sproul, *Reason to Believe* (Grand Rapids, MI: Lamplighter, 1982), 44.
11. John 3:16.
12. John 1:11–12.
13. Isaiah 59:2.
14. Romans 5:8.
15. Quoted in Assayas, 204.

Chapter 10

1. Ravi Zacharias, *Jesus among Other Gods* (Nashville: Word, 2000), 158.

2. Martha T. Moore and Dennis Cauchon, "Delay Meant Death on 9/11," *USA Today*, September 3, 2002.

3. Charles W. Colson, *Born Again* (Old Tappan, NJ: Chosen, 1976), 114.

4. Ravi Zacharias, *A Shattered Visage: The Real Face of Atheism* (Grand Rapids, MI: Baker, 2004), 155.

5. C. S. Lewis, *Mere Christianity* (San Francisco: Harper, 2001), 56.

6. Colson, 129.

7. Colossians 2:2–3 (Phillips).

8. Colossians 1:21–22 (NLT).

9. John 10:10 (NLT).

10. John 14:27 (NLT).

11. John 1:12 (NLT).

12. Ephesians 1:3–11 (Phillips).

13. 2 Corinthians 5:17 (NLT).

14. Hebrews 13:5.

15. Philippians 1:6.

Appendix A

1. 1 John 5:13.

2. Revelation 3:20; Hebrews 13:5.

3. Colossians 1:14; 1 John 1:9.

4. John 3:16; 1 John 5:11–13.

5. John 16:24; 1 John 5:14–15;

6. 2 Timothy 1:7; 1 Corinthians 10:13.

7. Ephesians 3:17; Hebrews 13:5.

8. Samantha Tidball, "Letting God Love Us," samtidball.blogspot.com.

9. 2 Corinthians 5:14–15.

ENDNOTES

Appendix B

1. 2 Peter 1:16 (NLT).
2. Will Durant, *Caesar and Christ*, vol. 3 of The Story of Civilization (New York: Simon & Schuster, 1972), 555.
3. Bruce M. Metzger, *The Text of the New Testament* (New York: Oxford University Press, 1992), 38–39, Note #2. This fragment (P52) of John's Gospel has been dated by most scholars to the first half of the second century. However, noted scholar Adolph Deissmann "was convinced that it was written well within the reign of Hadrian (AD 117–138) and perhaps even during the time of Trajan (AD 98–117)"
4. William F. Albright, *Recent Discoveries in Biblical Lands* (New York: Funk & Wagnalls, 1955), 136.
5. William F. Albright, "Toward a More Conservative View," *Christianity Today*, January 18, 1993, 3.
6. Quoted in Norman L. Geisler and Frank Turek, *I Don't Have Enough Faith to Be an Atheist* (Wheaton, IL: Crossway, 2004), 243.
7. Josh McDowell, *The New Evidence That Demands a Verdict* (Nashville: Thomas Nelson, 1999), 33–68.
8. Ibid., 38.
9. Metzger, 34.
10. John A. T. Robinson, *Can We Trust the New Testament?* (Grand Rapids, MI: Eerdmans, 1977), 36.

11. Quoted in McDowell, 36.
12. J. P. Moreland, *Scaling the Secular City* (Grand Rapids, MI: Baker, 2000), 134–57.
13. Quoted in Geisler and Turek, 256.
14. Moreland, 136–7.
15. Geisler and Turek, 276. See "Jesus.doc" at Y-Jesus.com/Evidence for other internal evidences for the New Testament.
16. D. James Kennedy, *Skeptics Answered* (Sisters, OR: Multnomah, 1997), 73.
17. Norman L. Geisler and Paul K. Hoffman, eds., *Why I Am a Christian* (Grand Rapids, MI: Baker, 2001), 150.
18. Ibid.
19. Metzger, 86.
20. Quoted in Josh McDowell, *The Resurrection Factor* (San Bernardino, CA: Here's Life Publishers, 1981), 9.

About Y-Jesus.com

DO YOU HAVE more questions about Jesus? Discover the facts on the Y-Jesus.com website with these articles:

"Was Jesus a Real Person?"
Demonstrates the historical
evidence for Jesus' existence

"Was There a Da Vinci Conspiracy?"
Exposes to the facts the best-selling
novel's attack on Jesus

"Is Jesus God?"
Explores why Jesus could not have
been just a good moral teacher

"Are the Gospels True?"
Examines the reliability of the New Testament

"WAS JESUS THE MESSIAH?"
Reveals how Jesus fulfilled hundreds of
Old Testament prophecies

"DID JESUS RISE FROM THE DEAD"
Investigates the historical evidence
for the resurrection of Jesus

"IS JESUS RELEVANT TODAY?"
Explains Jesus' relevance to our
lives now and in the future

Scan the QR code above with your
smartphone to access more content online.

WinePressPublishing
Great Books, Defined.

To order additional copies of this book call:
1-877-421-READ (7323)
or please visit our website at
www.WinePressbooks.com

If you enjoyed this quality custom-published book,
drop by our website for more books and information.

www.winepresspublishing.com
"Your partner in custom publishing."

CPSIA information can be obtained at www.ICGtesting.com
Printed in the USA
BVOW032044070213

312712BV00001B/3/P